Acclaim for **It's Y**~~OUR Future~~**...**

Make it a (

WINNER! 2012 "Most Important Futures Work"
Awarded by the Association of Professional Futurists

"In the introduction to his latest book... Wheelwright offers one of the most succinct explanations of the difference between prediction and foresight."

> Joe Tankersley, "Unique Visions" blog.

"It's Your Future..."highly recommended. It's a reference manual for a lifetime.

> Don Clifford, Author, *Ben Solomon*.

"...particularly useful for young professionals who are facing a multitude of choices in their career."

> Marcel Bullinga, Author, *Welcome to the Future Cloud*.

"It's all here with charts and diagrams...but more than that it's a remarkably concise picture of the obstacles that serious people encounter when trying to organize their lives."

> Mona D. Sizer, Author, *The Glory Guys*.

"Using **It's YOUR Future... Make it a Good One!** as a text in class again was a big success."

> Dr. Roy Pearson, William & Mary's Mason School of Business.

"This book offers insights into how futures methods work and is intended to help individuals develop a long term perspective not only in their personal lives but also in their careers. The book is written to be useful to people of all ages, from teenagers to octogenarians."

> Steve Saenz, Copernicus Radio.

Two workbooks

<u>at no cost</u>

The Personal Futures Workbook

and the

Small Business Foresight

written to use with

It's YOUR Future … Make it a Good One!

Both are available as free PDF downloads at
<u>www.personalfutures.net</u>.

The *Personal Futures Workbook* follows *It's YOUR Future*, chapter by chapter, to help you record information about your life, develop scenarios about plausible and possible futures, create a vision of your future, and create plans for the next ten years for yourself and your family.

The *Small Business Foresight* workbook also parallels *It's YOUR Future*, but applies everything you learn about the future to long-term planning for a small or medium size business. The same methods and tools used by international corporations, scaled down to fit any business.

It's YOUR Future

MAKE IT A GOOD ONE!

VERNE WHEELWRIGHT, PHD

Copyright © 2010 by Verne Wheelwright

Published by Personal Futures Network

Verne Wheelwright
1917 Guava Circle
Harlingen, TX 78552

verne@personalfutures.net
www.personalfutures.net

ISBN: 978-0-9788308-5-4
Ebook ISBN: 978-0-9788308-6-1

Library of Congress Control Number: 2010908080

Printed in the United States of America

Contents

Figures

Chapter 7

Chapter 8

Chapter 9

STEP TWO
Chapter 10

Chapter 11

Chapter 12

STEP THREE
Chapter 15

Chapter 16

Chapter 17

Chapter 18

Chapter 19

Acknowledgments

A great number of people have been involved in bringing this book to publication, but foremost is my wife, Betty, who encouraged me to go back to school, to enroll in research, and to write.

My foundation in the field of Foresight and Futures Studies is based primarily on the efforts of three educators, Dr. Peter Bishop, Dr. Oliver Markley, and Dr. Wendy Schultz at the University of Houston, Clear Lake. My dissertation research was guided by Graham May, Professor Jeffrey Gold, and Professor Eamonn Judge of Leeds Metropolitan University. My earliest writing on personal futures was greatly encouraged by Gitte Larsen, the editor at that time of *FO/futureorientation* published by the Copenhagen Institute of Futures Studies.

Initial drafts of this book were read by Erin King and Lindsay Pearson. The manuscript was read by author and editor of more than thirty books, Mona Sizer, by retired Professor of Futures Studies, Dr. Oliver Markley, and by Chancellor Professor of Business, Dr. Roy Pearson, who offered valuable advice and encouragement.

Introduction

EXPECT to be surprised.

First, you will be surprised to find how much you *can* know about your future.

Second, you will be surprised at how much *influence* you can have over your future.

Third, you will be surprised to find that you can discover and avoid many of the unpleasant surprises that are waiting in your future.

You can achieve all of this by simply thinking about your future in a systematic manner, and that is what this book offers. A system that leads you through the exploration of your future and then shows you how to decide on and achieve the future you want.

This is a simple, step-by-step process that has been used by thousands of people all over the world.

The final surprise will come when you realize that you are thinking in a different way. Really! You will find that the future has become a part of your everyday thoughts. That is how you acquire a long-term perspective on life and the world around you. It is a very valuable tool.

Whether you are young, old, or somewhere in between, you will learn something valuable about your future in this book. That's a promise.

Verne Wheelwright, PhD

CHAPTER 1

Everyone Wants to Know the Future!

FOR thousands of years of written history, people have wanted to know about the future.

They consulted witches, fortune tellers, palm readers and astrologists, but to no avail. Finally, in the twenty-first century, most of them gave up. In this electronic age, people finally realized that no one can really tell them the future. But …

Now it is possible. It is possible to understand and anticipate the future! It is even possible to influence or change the future. Not *all* of the future, but enough to be valuable.

In the 1950s and 1960s, think tanks and academics developed theories about anticipating the future. What was it that the think tanks found that the wizards and fortune tellers of earlier centuries had not? The answer seems so simple. The fortune tellers had focused on *the* future, assuming there was only one fixed, or preordained future.

The twentieth-century thinkers changed that main assumption. They were convinced that the future is *not* predetermined. That realization altered everything about the way we see the future.

Now, it became obvious that if the future is not fixed or predetermined, then more than one future must be available. Finally, they realized that it is possible to change the future through the actions we take in the present. This was a whole new way to look at the future!

Military and business organizations took those theories seriously and developed practical methods to explore and prepare for the future. The methods proved successful and spread into businesses and governments around the world. Shell Oil developed scenarios that anticipated the OPEC crisis of the 1970s, to their great benefit. Futurists wrote scenarios for South Africa that changed the expected future of that nation and led to a peaceful exchange of power. Futurists raised the alarm of the millennium bug in computer systems. Business and government responded in time to avoid a disruption.

To business, the military, and governments worldwide, the concept was clear. Methods for anticipating the future work. As a result, futures or foresight methods are now practiced around the world. As the result of recent research, these same methods have now been successfully scaled down to fit the life of one person—or one family. Anyone. This book will introduce you to futures methods and how they work; then it will lead you, step-by-step, through the personal futuring process in just three parts.

1. Look at your life and where you are now
2. Explore your futures with scenarios
3. Create your future—the future you want to live

As you follow this personal futuring process, you will be practicing the same methods and techniques that futurists have applied successfully for large organizations over the past several decades.

Let's look at just a little more about those three steps.

LOOK AT YOUR LIFE AND WHERE YOU ARE NOW

The first step in learning about your future is to look briefly at your past and your present, because they are the base from which you will launch into the future. Your map of the future will be based on biology and human experience over the centuries. You will learn about the six forces that are part of your daily life and how they will carry you through the events that you can expect to occur throughout your life.

That knowledge of your life will prepare you for the next section, exploring plausible futures.

EXPLORE YOUR FUTURES WITH SCENARIOS

"Exploring your future" may sound mysterious, but it is really quite practical. In this section you will develop scenarios that explore different types of futures, including the best, the worst, and the unexpected or "wild card" scenarios. These are all stories about you and what may happen in your life over the next ten years or more.

Create Your Future—The Future You Want to Live

Can you really do that? Create your future? Yes. You do that every day when you make decisions about what you are going to do in the days or weeks ahead. If you make plans for the weekend, register for school, make an airline reservation, you are changing or creating your future. Those are simple, short-term examples, but creating your long-term future is the same principle. First you must decide what you want to do. What do you want your future to be, for example, in ten years? Then you make a plan based on what you must do to achieve that future.

In reality, this futuring system is a guide that helps you think about your future in a systematic way. It has small, easy steps that add up to creating a future that you want.

In this busy, interactive world, changes happen fast, so you tend to react to whatever has your immediate attention. To some extent, the world around you is deciding your life. However, if you have a plan for your life, then as you make daily decisions, small as they may be, you will keep moving toward your plan and toward the future that you want for yourself.

Figure 1.1 - A diagram of a plan for achieving a future.

If you have a vision, a picture in your mind, of the future you would like to be living in ten years, you have created a long-term view of your life. That long-term view will put the small things that occur in your daily life in better proportion. You will find that minor irritations are just that—minor. They will be easier to accept, deal with, and move on from because they are not important in your long-term view. In other words, you will simplify your life.

You will probably not be able to follow a straight line from the present to the future, but if you have a vision of what you want in the future, that vision will provide a destination that you can be constantly moving toward. It is somewhat like tacking a sailboat into the wind. You may alter your course many times, but despite headwinds or obstacles, you continue to move toward your destination.

Figure 1.2 - Your route to the future may not follow a straight line, but having a vision of your long-term future will keep you moving in the right direction.

It really is that simple. Decide what your want for your future. Determine what you have to do to get there; then do it. Whether or not you make plans, you *will* create your own future, so it is worth whatever time you spend on planning to make your future a good one!

As you read through the chapters, you will probably want to try some of the exercises. Blank copies of the worksheets for each exercise are in the appendix of this book. There is also a workbook, *The Personal Futures Workbook,* available on my Web site, www.personalfutures.net, as a free download. You can download the workbook and save it in your computer, then fill in the worksheets to build your personal plan. You can make changes over the years or have multiple workbooks. Print them, if you wish. The choices are up to you.

Now, it is time to start exploring your future, beginning with step one.

Step One

Your first step toward the future is all about you. You will be learning about your life up to the present, understanding the forces that are changing your life, and recognizing some of the events that will occur in your future.

In this section, you will learn how to recognize and anticipate change. You will learn about six categories of forces that are continually introducing change into your life. You will also learn about five categories of forces that are changing the world around you.

The things you learn about yourself in this section will be your foundation for exploring and preparing for your futures.

CHAPTER 2

A Map to Your Future: Stages of Your Life

CONCEPT

YOU can learn a great deal about the future by understanding and exploring cycles, which are repetitive patterns that occur in nature and in your life. Familiar cycles include the daily cycle of morning, noon, and night; the seasonal cycle of spring, summer, winter, and fall; and the biological cycle of birth, reproduction, and death. The cycle you will explore in this chapter is the human life cycle, because it can tell you quite a bit about your future.

When you start on a long trip, it helps to have a map to show you where you are going and what you might encounter along the way. In this chapter you will be looking at your entire future, so you will start with a map of life. The adventurers and trailblazers who made the first maps of the physical world did not have much to guide them. They had to find their way; then they created a map for those who followed.

Fortunately, millions of people have gone through the experience of living. They left behind records and observations of their experiences over thousands of years, and their experience is your map. A very simple map of life would be just a straight line, starting with birth and ending with death.

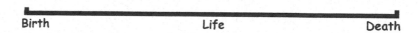

Birth   Life   Death

Figure 2.1 - A simple timeline of life.

To lead you through life, you will need a map with a little more detail than this timeline offers, and there are two good approaches to making that map. There is an Eastern version and a Western version of the map of life. The Eastern version tends to be more philosophical than the Western version, dividing life into four stages of about twenty years each.

The Western version is based more on biology and change; traditionally it has included seven or eight stages. We will use the Western version here because it offers more detail to help guide you through life.

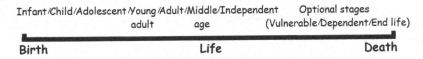

Figure 2.2 - A timeline of life divided into stages.
Each stage represents change in your life.

In this Western version, the first records of life stages were from the ancient Greeks. Those observations were passed up through the time of Shakespeare and into present theories of psychology. I have adjusted the stages slightly and redefined old age, since we are now living longer, healthier lives that go beyond the traditional stages. In that process, I have recognized three optional stages and added them to what used to be known as old age. The first seven stages of life are based largely on biology, while the three optional stages are based more on health and physical or mental condition.

As a map to your future, these stages have important values. The first is that each change from one stage to another represents a time of change in your life. That change is important, because change is what you look for when you explore the future. You want to know what is going to be different. If the future were going to be the same as the present, there would not be much interest in learning about the future, because there would be no mystery, no potential surprises. The point is that when you enter your next stage of life, you should expect change.

A second value of the life stages is that each stage represents a time interval, so you can anticipate how long you will be in this stage before the next big change. The intervals are not precise, but if you are anticipating change, you will be prepared to recognize and adjust to it. Think back to when you made the change from being a child to being an adolescent. The changes were gradual and took place over time and sometimes were surprising. At some point you realized that things were different; you were not a child any more. That is the way change will happen when you enter your next stage of life.

Finally, because you have experienced some life stages already, you have mental images of those stages. Can you picture yourself in those earlier stages? Can you create a mental image of each stage? Thinking about future life stages is the same process except that you don't have images from your own life. You have to start with images that you have of other people's lives, usually from observing their experiences.

Begin by reading the descriptions of ten life stages below. Decide what life stage you are in now and what stage you will be living in during most of the next ten years. Now, try to form a mental image of that stage of life. You probably know people who are living in that stage now, and you will be able to develop detailed images in your mind about that stage as you think more about your future.

Observing other people's lives in their present stages will help you to build images in your mind of what you may want in your life when you reach that stage, or what you may want to avoid. Look for role models, winners, and losers, and think about the differences. Then choose the images that you want to guide you to your future.

Understanding the life stages that are ahead of you or your family members will give you a long-term perspective on your life that will help you to antici-pate change and will prepare you for the stages ahead. Keep that thought in mind as you look at each of the life stages.

Ten Stages of Life

The first stage of life is the infant stage, which begins at birth and lasts through the first two years of life. In this stage, the infant's brain is developing, and the body is learning motor skills, starting with reaching and grasping and eventually leading to walking and talking. At first the infant is dependent upon his parents for nearly everything, but then he begins to take steps, liter-ally, toward independence.

The second stage of life is the child stage, which begins at age three and lasts through the ninth year. This is a stage of continued growth and mastery of motor skills. Children develop language skills, learn to socialize with other children, and begin formal schooling, participating in team sports and beginning to learn about life.

The third life stage is the adolescent stage, the teen years. The adolescent stage begins at ten and lasts through the nineteenth year; this stage includes puberty, hormonal changes, and growth spurts. Peer pressures and loyalties are important in this stage, as are the beginnings of independence and responsibility. This is also an age of risky behaviors that may result in injuries or long-term health effects. In some societies, adolescents complete their education, enter trades, and begin their families.

The fourth life stage is the young adult stage, from age twenty through twenty-nine. In some societies, this is the stage during which many of life's most important decisions are made, including decisions about the extent or completion of education, the start of work or a career, marriage, and the beginning of a family. The human brain completes its growth at about age twenty-two, and physical development of the body peaks at about age thirty.

The fifth stage of life, the adult stage, is from age thirty through thirty-nine. This is a time of being a parent to young and growing children as well as nurturing a growing career. Those two tasks sometimes conflict with each other. This may also be a time of difficult financial pressures, with a potential for divorce and remarriage. In some societies, professionals are just beginning their families in this stage. Physical growth is complete, but fitness may start to decline.

The sixth life stage, middle age, begins at age forty and lasts through the fifty-ninth year. This is the stage during which one's children become adults and start their own lives. It is also a time of young grandchildren. This is the stage when the first physical signs of aging appear in the form of wrinkles, bifocals, and menopause, yet for many, these are their peak earning years. Traditionally, at this stage, people start thinking about and planning for retirement, but as people live longer, healthier lives, that may change.

During this stage, many families find that they are still helping their adult children at the same time as they are helping their parents, who are now having health problems or are near the end of life. For planning, this stage can be divided into two ten-year parts: early and late middle age.

The seventh life stage is the independent stage, potentially the longest stage of your life. At sixty, people become independent elders, although most still feel young enough that they are not ready to be called elder. In this stage, people prepare for and eventually enter retirement. They may also become eligible for government social security funds and government health plans. For those with some financial security and reasonable health, this is an age of discretionary time, with fewer career or family obligations. Now, they can be busy doing the things they *want* to do.

Later in this stage, there is a potential for increasing and chronic health problems, although these are often manageable. Many people in this stage now feel that "seventy is the new fifty" because they feel as well and as capable at seventy as they did at fifty. Carrying this thought farther, as you plan for your long-term future, you should consider the possibility of living in the independent stage to age one hundred or beyond, as that goal is becoming more and more achievable.

Because this stage is not limited by chronological age, you can plan for ten years at a time, but it is important that you also make plans now for the last three stages of life. Not everyone goes through them, but once you enter one of these optional stages, you will find it much more difficult to plan or even make your own decisions, so it is important to have plans in place well before you enter one of these stages.

The remaining three stages are optional, as not everyone passes through them. These stages are all related to health rather than age, and as the general level of health improves, fewer people will enter these stages for lengthy periods.

The eighth life stage is the vulnerable stage, as individuals in this stage are vulnerable to becoming disabled. Although it is the stage most representative of what used to be called "old age," not everyone experiences the frailty or early dementia normally associated with this stage. The term vulnerable suggests that people in this stage are vulnerable to becoming dependent. They can no longer drive and may not be able to use electronic communication systems or public transportation. With a healthy spouse or caregiver, "vulnerables" can remain at home, but they may move to an assisted living facility. One reason this is an optional stage is that more people have learned about the long-term health benefits of exercise.

The dependent stage is also optional. Statistics suggest that less than 22 percent of people over age sixty (in the United States) are dependent on others for care; that is, they need help with the activities of daily living (ADLs) *every day*. The ADLs include the ability to get in and out of bed, walk, bathe, use the toilet, and feed oneself. Stated another way, more than 78 percent of people over age sixty in the United States are *not* considered disabled. The percentage of older people becoming disabled appears to be declining as people live longer and healthier lives. Dependent elders require some help from a caregiver at home, or they may live in an assisted living facility or be cared for in a nursing home. The length of this stage varies with individuals and conditions. Some people who are dependent have suffered a stroke, heart attack, or cancer, and some of those individuals return to the independent stage. Others may have Alzheimer's or other disease that has made them permanently dependent.

Many people do not experience the end-of-life stage. This stage usually lasts less than six months, partly because of Medicare's policy (in the United States) regarding payment for hospice care. Terminal patients may receive hospice or palliative care, which is care to make the person comfortable and free of pain without measures to cure the disease or condition. People receiving hospice care are usually spared the trauma of emergency life-saving procedures. End-of-life care can be provided in a patient's own home, a nursing home, or a hospice facility.

The table below summarizes the ten stages.

Life Stage	Characteristics of Life Stage
Infant	Birth through 2 years. Dependent, brain developing, learning motor skills, and sensory abilities.
Child	3–9 years. Growing and mastering motor skills and language. Learning to play and socialize. Continued growth, formal school, and organized activities.
Adolescent	10–19 years. Growth spurts. Puberty brings hormonal changes and reactions. Strong emotions often rule decisions. Risks for injury, alcohol, drugs, tobacco, etc. In some societies, education ends and marriage and family decisions are made.
Young Adult	20–29 years, Completing higher education and beginning career and family. Potential coping and financial pressures.
Adult	30–39 years. Managing family and career growth. Increasing numbers of couples are starting families in this stage. Continued coping pressures.
Middle age	40–60 First signs of aging and effects of lifestyle; menopause, children are leaving the nest, grandchildren arrive, career peak. Aging parents may require help.

Independent Elder	60 onward. More signs of aging and lifestyle effects. Eligible for Social Security, Medicare (United States), pensions. Retirement. More discretionary time and opportunities for travel, hobbies, and sports. Some health problems and medications. May be caring for a spouse or others.
Vulnerable Elder (Optional)	Beginning frailty, cognitive or multiple health problems. Require some assistance. Stop driving. Possible move to assisted living facility. This stage is optional, but in the past it was the image of old age.
Dependent Elder (Optional)	Requires daily care. Unable to perform all personal functions. Possible move to nursing home. This stage is also optional.
End of Life (Optional—Up to six months)	Diagnosed with terminal condition or the final stage of a disease. May require hospice care, hospitalization, or nursing home care. This stage may be very brief.

Figure 2.3 - A table showing seven life stages and three optional stages.

As a map, this is pretty rough, yet a lot of information about your future can be seen in these ten stages. Just having the knowledge of the stages and adding your personal images of stages yet to come will give you a surprising amount of information about your future.

IMAGES OF THE FUTURE

What do I mean when I refer to personal images or *your* images of the future? When someone says "middle aged," "teenager," or "retired," do you get a mental picture? Can you visualize someone you know at one of those times of life?

Now, expand that thought. For the stages that are still ahead of you, what is the image you have of life in that stage? Do you usually think of each of these stages as positive, negative, or balanced?

Look at the list of life stages in figure 2.3 again and pick the first complete life stage that is still ahead of you. What is your current image of that life stage? What do you know about this stage? Perhaps you remember when your parents, acquaintances, or friends passed through this stage. Many of the characteristics of the stage will be the same for you as they are for them. Visualize people you know who are in this stage of life now. Where are they in their careers? What are their interests? What is their financial condition? Where do they live? Are they healthy? How do you see their family life? Answering these questions will begin to give you a picture of that stage of life.

Next, imagine yourself in this stage and ask the same questions. The answers will move you from developing general images of a future life to developing an image of *your* future in that life stage. You are putting yourself into your picture of this future life stage.

As you create images of your future, add in family members and close friends. Calculate how old each person will be during the years for which you are creating images. This should help to sharpen your focus. It may be hard to imagine your ten-year-old children as parents with small children of their own in fifteen years, but that is likely to be the case. Can you see yourself as a grandparent? Or, if you are already a grandparent, as a great grandparent?

What will your community, your neighborhood, and your home look like ten to fifteen years from now? Will everything be the same, better, or worse? Is this where you want to be, or would you rather live somewhere else? What will you look like in ten to fifteen years? Depending on your age now, you may be heavier, less physically fit, and grayer, as these are pretty common changes as people age. Health problems may start appearing during middle age. You can accept any image you see, or you can take action now and over the coming years to change any of these images.

At this point, you have started with a background image of a life stage, then added yourself and your family in varying situations and activities to make multiple images. You can make adjustments along the way that will make the image more desirable, but you now have multidimensional images of one stage in your future life. This is the real advantage of developing images of the future. *The images can be changed, and so can the future.* You can imagine the future you want and change or discard the images you do not want. It is all part of the concept of choosing preferred futures.

Understanding the descriptions and images of life's stages will help you to understand the lives and futures of your family members and other people around you. But, before you move on to exploring the lives of people close to you, it will be helpful through the rest of this book for you to know which life stage you are in now and which stage you will move into next.

Knowing those two stages will be important as you go into the next chapter, where you will learn about the people who have the power to change your life.

CHAPTER 3

The People in Your Future

CONCEPTS

YOUR future will be influenced by the people who are involved in or who have an interest in your life—your stakeholders. In turn, you will influence the lives of your family and the people around you.

Your future will be also influenced by major events that occur during the first twenty years of life. Your generation of peers and cohorts, people of similar age and experiences, will also be influenced by those same events.

Who will be the people in your life ten years from now, and how will they affect your future between now and then? People *will* be important in your life, but who will they be? And why?

First, you will look at the stakeholders in your life and your future. Then you will learn something about your generation and about each of the generations you are living with now and in the future.

STAKEHOLDERS

Futurists use the term stakeholder to identify people who:

- Have an interest in your life
- Have the power to change or impact your life
- May be impacted by events in your life
- May be impacted by your decisions or actions

Obviously, close family members such as your parents, siblings, spouse, and children are stakeholders in your life, but there are other people, including teachers and mentors, who can influence or impact your future too. On the other side of that description are stakeholders who may be influenced or impacted by you and your actions or by events in your life.

How do stakeholders impact your life? When children are born, injured, get sick, get married, or have children of their own, they impact their parent's life. When family members are seriously injured or die, they impact your life. When someone makes you happy or miserable for a long time, he or she impacts your life. The good and bad things that impact close family members will also impact you. You will most likely share major life events with these people, whether those events are successes or failures, emotional ups and downs, or just experiences.

How will you impact other people's lives? Turn most of the events that would impact you around, and you are impacting someone's life. When you were a child, all the good and bad events that occurred in your life impacted your parents' lives. Now, if you encourage, coach, or mentor someone, especially your own child, you are making an impact on that person's life. Family members and close friends are the first people who come to mind when we think of stakeholders, but there are also stakeholders outside your family. Conversely, if you are in a position to hire, promote, or fire people, you are a stakeholder in their lives.

Who has an interest in your life? The diagram below suggests a few categories of potential stakeholders.

These are pretty broad categories, but as you think about them, you will see how people in each of these categories can be stakeholders in your life. Even faceless organizations can become very personal if they provide something you need or want something from you. Governments at all levels impact your life by raising taxes or making changes in your community. Business and financial organizations can be very persuasive when offering their services—but ruthless if you have a problem making payments. So there is value in understanding the perspectives and motivations of your stakeholders.

As you think about your stakeholders, keep asking yourself, "How can this person or organization impact my life in either a positive or a negative way? What might motivate them in either case?"

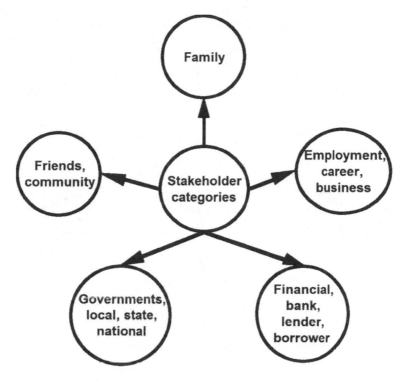

Figure 3.1 - Potential stakeholder categories.

In addition to knowing who your individual stakeholders are, it is helpful to know where each of your individual stakeholders is in their own lives now and where they will be in the future. If you have children who are in high school now, their lives will change substantially in the next few years. As they become young adults, they will be making decisions about completing their education, starting careers, moving into their own home, starting marriages, and starting families. Each of those decisions will probably impact your life.

If you are young, be aware of the life stages your parents are in now, and think about the stages in which they will be ten and twenty years from now. How will those changes affect them, and how will they affect you?

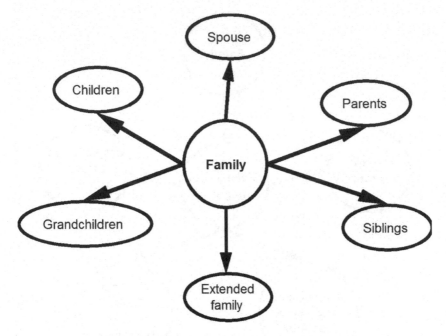

Figure 3.2 - Categories of family members.

It is easy to anticipate some of the things that will be happening in your children's lives, because you have been through those life stages and some of those experiences. Even so, each of their successes or disasters will have some impact on your life. At the same time, you may find that over the years you and your spouse will be impacted by events in your parents' lives. Aging and illness, for example may compel you to help multiple parents: your spouse's and your own.

Who else may be a stakeholder in your life? A very close friend, an important advisor or mentor, possibly an employer, or anyone you think might impact your life, or vice versa.

Now that you have recognized your stakeholders, ask yourself what stage of life each is in at the present. What stage is next and when? In what stage will each of these people be ten years from now? These questions add up to the important question, "What impact will the changes in each stakeholder's life have on you?"

Beyond the individuals who may impact your life, there will also be organizations that may have impacts on you and your family. Obviously your employer is in a position to influence your future. Your religious organization, your mortgage holder and other lenders, your bank, your investment advisor, national or local governments, and others are also in a position to cause change in your life.

Although all of these categories of stakeholders seem like a lot to think about, this is important. As you think about the next ten years or more, be aware of your stakeholders in each category and how each might impact your life. The 2008 financial crisis is a good example of why you should be aware of organizations and institutions that may be in a position to impact your life, either in a positive or negative way. In the 2008 crisis, one of the problems was predatory organizations, but you cannot assume that predators are your only risk. A fair, even benevolent organization can have negative impacts on your life if it is having problems of its own.

Now that you have explored your stakeholders, you can bring in the time element and add ten years to your age. Does that change anything? How do any of these relationships change? You and everyone in your family will be ten years older, most of you in another stage of life. There may be new members in your family: children, in-laws, grandchildren. Your boss or your mentor may be retired or with different companies then. Does that change anything for you?

Will changes in your own life affect relationships with some of your stakeholders? Very likely. If you retire, many if not most of your relationships related to your work will fade and vanish. Whatever position or role you have in your career will end. If you move to a different city, many of your close friendships will fade while you slowly build new friendships in your new community.

Over the next ten years, which of your stakeholders will graduate, get married, get divorced, be promoted or fired, move away, retire, become very ill, or die? How will those events impact you? Would knowing of these events in advance make any of them easier to deal with? How do you keep track of all these people and where they are in their lives?

Here are three possibilities for keeping track of stakeholder's ages and the stages of their lives:

- You can use the worksheet in the appendix of this book or *The Personal Futures Workbook*, a free download at www.personalfutures. net.
- You can use a formatted Excel worksheet, also a free download at www.personalfutures.net.

- You can make a chart on paper or in your computer using the example below as a model.

Year	Your age	Spouse age	Oldest child	Youngest child	Oldest parent	Youngest parent	Others
Name							
2010							
2011							
2012							
2013							

Figure 3.3 - A partial worksheet from the *Personal Futures Workbook*.

Any of these worksheets is a good place to list your key stakeholders and their present ages in one document. The Excel spreadsheet offers lots of space and instantly calculates future ages and stages up to age 100. Whether you use a worksheet or rely on your memory, the important thing is that you stay aware of your stakeholders and of the events that are occurring in their lives that might impact your future.

GENERATIONS

The news media frequently uses labels to refer to different generations, such as Boomers, Gen X, Millennials, and others. Since you and your family members each belong to a generation, you may find it interesting or helpful to know something about the theory or history behind these names.

To the best of my knowledge, this interest started with a book titled *Generations,* written in the early 1990s by two historians, Neil Strauss and William Howe. My brief interpretation of their theory is that children generally tend to turn away from some of their parents' beliefs and attitudes—such as their beliefs on raising children. That difference in beliefs is equivalent to about a quarter of a turn. This happens with each generation, so that every fourth generation will complete a cycle, and that generation will have beliefs and attitudes that are similar to those of the fourth generation earlier.

The authors of *Generations* also saw patterns of common, impressive events that occurred in different age groups as the result of wars, large technology changes, or major economic or social changes that tended to imprint a generation, giving it an identity and a common emotional or intellectual bond with other people who shared the same experiences. From there, Strauss and Howe set out to identify generational groups, or cohorts, throughout history.

The authors concluded that the length of a generation is *about* twenty years and that there is a sequence of four generational types, described with current examples as follows:

- Idealist generations—dominant, inner-fixated, increasingly indulged youths; narcissistic adults (the boomers).
- Reactive generations—recessive, underprotected, criticized youths mature into risk-taking, alienated adults (generation X).
- Civic generations—dominant, increasingly protected youths unite into a heroic and achieving cadre of adults (the millennials).
- Adaptive generations—recessive, overprotected, and suffocated youths mature into risk averse, conformist adults (the silent generation).

Six living generations are shown, along with their birth years and their generational type, in the following table.

Generation	Birth years	Generational Type	Formative or Imprinting events
G. I.	1901–1924	Civic	Autos, WWI, Aircraft, Depression, WWII, Postwar reconstruction
Silent	1925–1942	Adaptive	WWII childhood, atom bomb, Cold war, TV, Korean war, Sputnik, moon landing.
Boomer	1943–1960	Idealist	Dr. Spock, TV, Vietnam War, drugs, JFK, civil rights, Woodstock

Gen X	1961–1981	Reactive	Iran hostages, Pres. Reagan shot, MTV, Hip-hop, Berlin wall fell, computers and Internet
Millennial	1982–2003	Civic	Chosen children, Clinton scandals, computers in school, 9/11, Iraq wars, Columbine, Afghanistan war, 2008 recession.
Global*	2004–2025	Adaptive	Iraq, Afghanistan wars, 2008 recession, global economy, global communication. *Not named by Strauss and Howe. My term.

Figure 3.4 - Six currently living generations and a few events that shaped each generation.

Each of your family members and friends is in one of these generational groups, and you can probably recognize some of the characteristics described by Strauss and Howe. Not everyone fits neatly into a category, but as generalized groups, these seem to work pretty well and will give you some clues as to the generational mindsets of people around you.

Now you know about some of the people who will be in your future. The next chapter will explore the trends and forces that will bring change into your life, particularly over the next ten years.

CHAPTER 4

Trends and Forces: Anticipating Change in Your Life

CONCEPT

THE future is about change, because change is what makes the future different from the present. That is why people want to know about the future. They want to know what will be different, what will change. Change in your life is brought about by forces, the forces that exist in your life as well as the forces in the world around you.

One of the most important things I learned in several years of research is that everyone lives life on multiple levels, simultaneously balancing or managing each level. I calculate six levels, or domains, that I also treat as the major groups of forces in our lives. During any day, you are dealing with all six of these categories of forces. Some may be in the background, but they are still in your life, and when one force moves into the foreground and requires your attention, you deal with it. That force may retreat into the background again or may keep your attention for awhile until something else becomes more important.

WHAT IS A FORCE?

A force is a power that influences you or causes you to take action that brings about change. In your personal life, anything that motivates you or causes you to take action is a force. There are forces and sub-forces that move through your life and, in many cases, move or motivate you to act. When these forces pressure you or motivate you, they are driving forces in your life, or drivers. In personal futures, we recognize six categories or domains of forces that are common to all people and are a part of every person's life from birth through death. The six categories of forces in your personal life include:

Activities: All the things you do, including school, work, sports, hobbies, religion, and other activities.

Finances: Everything to do with your finances, including income, expense, investments, insurance, credit cards, debt, assets, and taxes.

Health: Your physical and mental health, including health care, nutrition, exercise, medications, and prevention of illness or injury.

Housing: Your home as well as your neighborhood, community, country, region, and climate.

Social: Your relationships with family, friends, acquaintances, coworkers, advisors, and other people.

Transportation or mobility. Your various transportation needs and the methods available, including walking, personal transport, and public transportation.

What I am suggesting here is that your life can be divided into six parts and that everything happening in your life will be in one of these six domains.

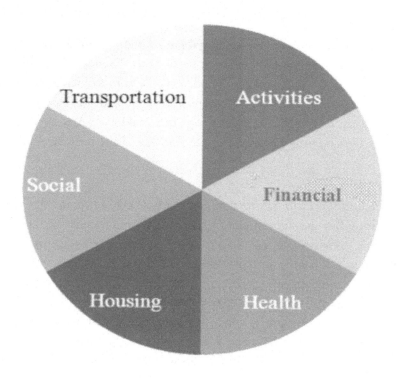

Figure 4.1 - Your life in six parts; your six personal domains.

Now, take a closer look into those six personal domains!

Activities

The activities domain covers the things that you *do* in life, and those activities change with age and the different stages of life. Children play games and learn team sports. Teens play individual and team sports, and adults move on to individual sports. Children, teens, and early twenties are in school; then by their midtwenties they are starting work or careers that last into their sixties or later. Religion can be an important part of life at any age. As people enter their sixties or approach retirement, they gain more discretionary time to travel or enjoy personal sports, hobbies, and other pursuits.

Finances

The finances domain covers everything related to your money. Income, expenses, debt, credit cards, and assets are obvious. Then add in your savings, investments, and retirement funds and taxes. Be sure to include your mortgage, as that will influence your future when it is paid off. Various types of insurance can be your hedge against large financial losses. Any of these financial forces can become a driving force in your life, either positive or negative.

Health

The health domain is one that many people take for granted while they are healthy. But the normal daily hygiene of washing your hands, brushing your teeth, exercising, eating a balanced diet, and bathing is a routine that can extend your health and your life. This domain covers all of that—your medical care, medications, screenings, checkups, and the risks you take with your body, including what you breathe. In your sixties, you may experience more need for health care and start paying a price in your physical well being for whatever areas of your health you have neglected or abused. One other thing. Even after retirement age, living a healthy lifestyle can improve your life. Longevity is a part of the health domain and is a dimension of life that seems to be changing, so at some point you may be looking forward to a much longer life than you expected. The best preparation for longevity is maintaining your physical and mental health.

Housing

The housing domain begins with your home, but includes the neighborhood, community, and country in which you live. The climate in your region is also a factor, as housing needs vary greatly between warm and cold climates.

Social

The social domain begins with close family and friends and expands outward to all of the people with whom you interact in your work or your community, including all of your stakeholders. On a larger scale, language, communication, and culture are also a part of the social domain because they are part of how you interact with others.

Transportation

The transportation domain includes all available means of mobility, beginning with walking, which is the primary transportation for a large part of the world's population. From there, add animals (horses, camels, oxen, even elephants), bicycles, wheelchairs, motorcycles, cars, and boats as personal transportation. Finally, include public transportation: taxis, buses, trains, ships, and airplanes.

Sometimes in workshops people ask how transportation can be a force in our lives. In simplest terms, our food and water generally do not come to us; we have to either live near them, go to them, or have them delivered to us. Transportation allows us to live in one area, work in another, and buy our food, merchandise, and services in other places, or have them delivered. You will probably recognize this force most quickly when it is not available (the car won't start) or when it becomes burdensome (a long daily commute).

That, very briefly, describes the six categories of internal forces in your life. Now, you will explore trends and trend lines, the diagrams that show how these forces change over a period of time, and how you can recognize and anticipate those changes.

Why should you care about trends and forces?

If you are aware of change (a trend) in your life, you can develop strategies and take actions to take advantage of the trend or to prevent the trend from running over you.

WHAT IS A TREND?

Futurists and the media talk about trends a lot. But what are these trends, and what do they mean to you personally?

Trends indicate change, and change is what makes the future different from the present. The reason people are interested in the future is that they want to know what will change.

Most of the trends that you will hear about in the media and from futurists are the big-picture trends, and they generally fall into five categories: social change, technological change, economics, ecology, and politics. These trends are important and will affect the world you live in, but you will consider those external trends and forces in a later chapter. In this chapter, you will focus on the trends and forces in your personal life: the internal forces.

A trend is an indicator of change and of the *direction* a change force is moving. A trend line is an image, usually a line derived from time-series data such as population statistics over a period of years. The line shows the direction a force is moving and whether the force is increasing or decreasing.

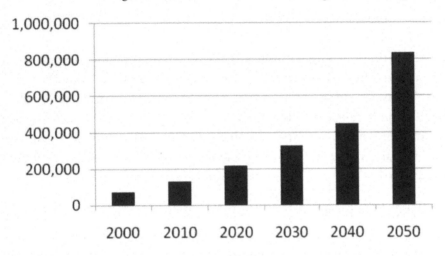

Figure 4.2 - An example of time-series data. This is a projection of the number of centenarians in the United States from 2000 through 2050. The time period is from 2000 to 2050, the series is in ten year intervals, and the data are the number of centenarians at each interval.

The trend in this graph is upward, showing increasing numbers of centenarians each decade. In figure 4.3, a trend line has been drawn across the data points to better illustrate the change that is taking place. The trend line is indicating the *direction* of change as well as the *speed* of change. Notice how the line turns more sharply upward between 2040 and 2050, indicating that the numbers of centenarians are expected to grow more rapidly.

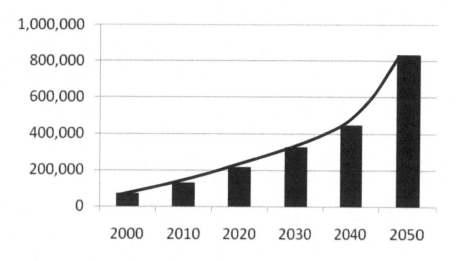

Figure 4.3 - The same data as figure 4.2, but with a trend line added.

A trend line is a picture (or a drawing) representing change in data over a period of time. Once you have a trend line showing change from the past to the present, you can start thinking about the future of that trend. Where will the trend line go next? Will it go up or down? Why?

If you are familiar with the data that lie under the trend line, you can probably make some pretty good guesses about the direction of the trend line over the next year or two. But the farther into the future you look, the more uncertain the future is likely to become. The possibilities for change become greater as you move farther away from the present.

Whenever you are looking at a trend line or extending a trend line into the future yourself, it is valuable to keep asking, "What could cause the line to change its direction? Or not?"

In most cases, straight lines oversimplify the image of change, but aging is one example of a true linear trend. Aging is also a dominant trend in everyone's life. Every day, every week, every year, everyone gets a little older. That force carries us from one life stage to the next, into the future. Unlike other forces, aging is constant. It does not change directions or fluctuate. The *effects* of aging may change or differ from one person to another, but aging itself remains the same. For that reason, people view aging through its effects, the stages of life, and the six personal domains.

For individuals, aging is different in another important way when thinking about the future. By different, I mean different from organizations. For businesses, governments, and other organizations, year-by-year aging is not an important force when thinking about the future in the same way as for individuals. Organizations experience change over time, but individuals experience change *because* of time.

POSSIBLE, PLAUSIBLE, AND PROBABLE

Anything is possible, but ...

Futurists have to give considerable thought to possibilities, plausibilities, and probabilities—events that may happen in the future. How do you sort these out or even try to define them? Here is a simple diagram that will help to clarify the differences.

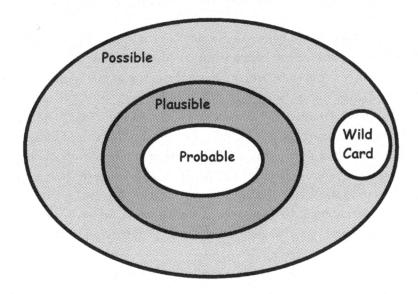

Figure 4.4 - A diagram showing the relationships between *possible*, *plausible*, *probable*, and wild card futures and events. You will use these concepts of possible, plausible, probable, and wild cards all through this book.

The large, outer oval represents everything that can possibly happen in your life. If you apply this diagram to your life and future, this circle contains all of the events that could possibly happen in your life and in your future. This includes high-probability events, low-probability events, and everything in between.

The next smaller oval is labeled "Plausible." Within this oval are the events that have a reasonable chance of happening in our life. Some plausible events will actually happen and others may not, but they are plausible. For example, for most people, meeting the queen or the president or any other world-famous person is highly unlikely, but it is possible. But if you belong to certain social circles, or if you accomplish something outstanding, then such a meeting might become plausible.

Inside the plausible area is one more oval, labeled "Probable." Within this oval are the events that will probably happen in your life. Completing secondary school is probable for most people, but earning a college or university degree is, for many, only plausible, not probable.

The probable circle contains the events that you should be aware of and for which you should be planning, particularly those events that will have a strong impact on your life. Some events are highly probable, like birthdays, but they do not have much impact on your life. As you will see in later chapters, personal strategic planning will focus on the events that both have a high probability of occurring and will have a strong impact on your life.

The wild card circle is off by itself. Events in this circle are neither plausible nor probable. Wild card events are low-probability, high-impact events like winning the lottery or being hit by a meteor and are not likely to occur. You will have a chance to look at these events in some detail in the section on developing wild card scenarios. In addition, some low-probability, high-impact events will be included in your contingency plan, which you will create later.

This chapter has focused on defining or clarifying terms or concepts so that you will be able to use these terms easily throughout the book. In the next chapter, you will examine trends and forces in your own life and will learn how to extend trend lines into your futures.

CHAPTER 5

Forces in Your Life:
Past, Present, and Future

CONCEPT

THE forces in your life can be understood, anticipated, and changed. Once you understand what forces exist in your life, you will be able to track where those forces have been in your past and anticipate their plausible directions in the future. It is a core concept among futurists that actions taken in the present can impact or change the directions of forces, resulting in changes in the future.

Now that you know about the forces in your life, what can you do with them? How do you use them to see where your future is going?

The answer is simple. Follow the forces that are in your life now and extend them into the future. But, how do you do that? Futurists use trend lines to visualize the effects and impacts of different forces over time. They gather statistics about a force or its effects and draw a trend line. The trend line indicates the amount, direction, and speed of change up to the present. The futurist then tries to determine where the trend will go in the future. The trend may turn upward, it may continue to follow its present trajectory, or it may turn downward. The speed of change may slow or accelerate. Trend lines illustrate all of these changes.

One method of extending trend lines into the future is extrapolation. In extrapolating from a trend line, a common approach is to extend two lines from the present into the future. They include a positive or best plausible projection and a negative or worst plausible projection.

You may be asking yourself, "How do I apply this concept to my life?"

That is what this chapter is about: visualizing your past, present, and future.

VISUALIZING YOUR DOMAINS

How do you see the changes in your life, whether in the past, present, or future? One answer is to create your own trend lines. As mentioned earlier, trend lines are usually based on statistics, or measurements. But how do you measure your life? That is the problem I came up against when I was conducting research into personal futures. What should I measure?

First, I concluded that measuring "life" was too general. I had already identified the six domains, so that was a logical place to start. Measure the domains. More specifically, measure the *quality of life* in each of the six domains.

- Activities
- Financial
- Health
- Housing
- Social
- Transportation

As for the quality-of-life measure, I started with a scale of one to five, or from very low quality to very high quality, then measured in ten-year periods, as in figure 1.

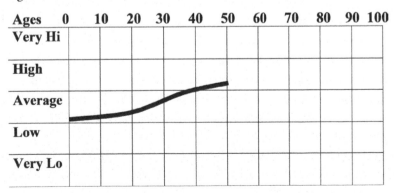

Figure 5.1 - An example of a personal trend line. This line shows how one person's life in one domain has changed over the years.

Once you start creating your own trend lines, what do you look for? Primarily, you will be looking for change, particularly in the past few years. Is your trend line moving up, down, or staying level? How fast is the line changing? Figure 5.1 shows a trend line that is rising since birth, and continues to rise during the last ten years. Notice that from age twenty to age thirty, the line rises faster. The speed of change has accelerated.

One of the advantages of creating trend lines for each domain is that you will recognize change more quickly within the shorter period of a domain than you may over the longer period of your whole life. By looking at six different parts of your life, you will be able to recognize which parts of your life are changing and whether those changes are positive or negative. Once you recognize what is changing in your life, you will be able to make decisions or develop strategies to improve your life and your future.

HOW DO YOU MAKE A TREND LINE?

In a blank chart like the one below, simply select the quality level (Very low to Very high) during each ten-year period of your life. Here is a point where your workbook will be helpful, as there are blank charts in the workbook that will help you create your graphs. The basic format is:

Ages	0	10	20	30	40	50	60	70	80	90	100
Very Hi											
High											
Average											
Low											
Very Lo											

Figure 5.2 - Graph format for plotting your quality of life at different ages. Graph forms and instructions are in the appendix, or you may download *The Personal Futures Workbook* (free) at www.personalfutures.net.

There are blank charts and detailed instructions in the appendix of this book for each of your personal domains. Each of these blank graphs is designed for you to draw a line that expresses your opinion about the quality of your life in that domain from your birth to today. Obviously, this graph is not designed for precision, and precision is *not* expected or desired. You can accomplish all this on any piece of paper, even on the back of a envelope. This is simply a way for you to draw a picture (line) of how you feel about the quality of your life in each of your six personal domains. That line will be your base, your launching point into your future.

In my workshops, this is the point where someone asks, "How do I mark the square?" The answer is, "Any way you want to." Some people make an X, some draw a line, and others make ten dots in a square, one for each year. They are all right. Whatever looks right to you will be fine.

When you have marked each column up to your present age, draw a line from the first mark to the second and on through each mark. Once you have drawn your line (this is a trend line) in each domain representing your life up to the present, you will have a foundation for projecting into your future in each domain.

LOOKING INTO YOUR FUTURE

Now that you can visualize the directions of the forces in your life at the present, you are ready to look at your future. This involves extending the trend lines in each of your domains ten years into the future. For each domain, you will draw two lines into the future. One line will represent the *best plausible* future for that domain, and the second will represent the *worst plausible* future for that domain.

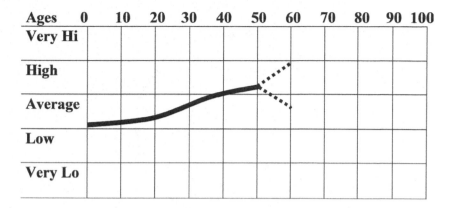

Figure 5.3 - A trend line extended to show the best plausible (upper) and worst plausible (lower) potential futures for the next ten years.

THE CONE OF UNCERTAINTY

Notice that the two lines projecting into the future form a cone. That is because the lines extending into the future are going into the unknown. As you travel away from the present into the future, the uncertainty increases, so the lines spread farther apart because more plausible events can occur as the future becomes more uncertain. Futurists call the area between the two lines the "cone of uncertainty." This area is important because the lines you have created form boundaries on your plausible futures.

Think about your life right now. Unless you are at a big transition point, like just about to graduate or to begin retirement, you probably know what you'll be doing, where you'll be living, what your health will be, and other things about your life for the next year or two. Three to five years will raise some questions, but the possibilities for change or surprises keep increasing every year. That explains why the two lines tend to spread apart as they go farther away from the present and into the future.

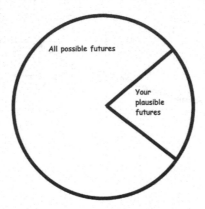

Figure 5.4 - The circle represents your possible futures over any given period of time. The wedge represents the plausible futures over the same time period.

As you can see from the diagram, you have narrowed the area of the future that you need to explore. You have put boundaries on your plausible futures.

Wild Cards

What about the rest of the circle in figure 5.4, the *implausible* futures? These are the futures that are not plausible but could occur because they are *possible*—like winning the lottery.

Futurists define wild cards as low-probablity, high-impact events. Wild card events occur in the areas outside the cone of plausibility and can be either positive or negative. Wild cards will be discussed in detail in chapter 7, "Life Events."

Projecting into the Future

Your personal domains are smaller segments of your life, so you may be aware of specific risks or opportunities that may occur in one of your domains. For example, you may expect a promotion at work in two years that would bring changes into your life. You might anticipate getting married or feel there is a risk of divorce. The point is that your trend lines don't have to be straight lines or even gentle curves. They can reflect known, plausible risks or opportunities.

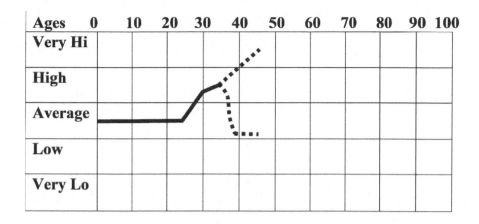

Figure 5.5 - One individual's graph reflecting risks and opportunities over the next ten years in one domain.

In the graph above, this person lived a very average life in this domain for twenty-five years, but upon graduation from college entered a very rewarding career, which raised her quality of life substantially. Looking ahead, this career should provide a very high quality of life (upper line). But there are risks due to a changed economy. Those risks would probably occur during the next few years (lower line), but their impacts could continue. This simply illustrates that you can reflect any possibilities in your charts, both positive and negative.

In short, your projections probably will not look like the classic cone of uncertainty because we have divided your life into six parts. Looking at your life in sections encourages you to think specifically about each part of your life, narrowing your focus on the future. In addition, you are encouraged to insert specific knowledge about the apparent or plausible risks that exist that might impact your future.

The emphasis here is on plausible. Consider the positive events that could reasonably occur over the next ten years in each domain. You are expected to be optimistic, but keep your projections within the plausible range. What could happen in a domain that would increase your quality of life and cause the upper line to rise higher? Or what would keep it from rising? Keep asking yourself, "What are the best things I can reasonably expect to happen in this domain?"

In the health domain, for example, humans reach a physical peak at about age thirty, so if you are already at your physical peak, the best you can expect is to maintain your present health. Your projection into the future would be a flat line because your best plausible projection would be maintaining the health you have now.

Domain	Common forces or sub-domains
Activities	Education, training Career, work Sports, hobbies Travel Religion
Finances	Income Investments Retirement funds Expenses Debt, credit cards Insurance Taxes
Health	Physical and mental condition Diet Exercise Medical treatment or care Medications
Housing	Home Community Nation, region Climate
Social	Family Friends Community Advisors
Transportation	Mobility Personal Public National or international

Figure 5.6 - Each of the six personal domains can be divided into forces or sub-domains such as these examples. Any of these sub-domains can be charted in the same manner as the domains.

DOMINANT FORCES

Throughout your life, usually two of the six domains will be dominant during any time period, but these dominant domains may change some from one life stage to the next. Moreover, the forces within a domain may change in importance. I will give just a little explanation here, but the question you will want to answer at the end of the chapter is, "Which of the six personal domains are likely to dominate your future over the next ten years?"

The reason for this question is that in step two of your futuring process, you will explore your alternate futures by constructing scenarios, and the driving forces in your life will determine the directions of the scenarios.

A driving force in your life pushes you to take action, whether positive, negative, offensive, or defensive. For most people, school, work, and careers force us to get up in the morning and be somewhere nearly every day. These same forces keep us at our duties for a period of time and sometimes pressure us to make choices between work and family.

What force causes people to go to work? Primarily, the need or desire for income. The income from working satisfies their needs for food and shelter as well as many other things. There are other forces involved with work and careers, such as the feelings of accomplishment or the desire for power that may motivate people as well.

Which domains are dominant in your life? Think about each of the personal domains and ask yourself which domain dominates your life right now. When you have to make choices, which domain wins? For most people, from childhood through middle age, the dominant domains are the activities domain and the social domain, which in turn are driven by their career (or school) and their family. Late in middle age or early in the independent stage, the health domain becomes dominant.

These are generalizations, but the important thing is that you think about and recognize the forces and domains that are influencing your life, now and in your future.

In this chapter we have focused on your personal domains because that is where your personal decisions help to determine your future. In the next chapter, you will take a close look at the big-picture forces, the forces in the world around you that may also shape your life and your future.

CHAPTER 6

Forces That Shape Your Worlds: Global, National, and Local

CONCEPT

THE forces that drive change in the world around you can also be anticipated and understood. Simply understanding and being aware of these forces and how they might impact your life provides an opportunity to develop strategies for dealing with those impacts, whether positive or negative.

How do you deal with the forces in your life that you cannot influence or control? Futurists find the answer to that question in one word.

Anticipation.

If you anticipate what may happen in the world around you, you can prepare. You can take a defensive position and minimize the impacts or damage, much as you might prepare for a hurricane or other natural disaster. You can also take an offensive or proactive position, profiting from the big changes that occur in your world. In 2008, not everyone suffered financial losses. Some individuals anticipated the downturn and withdrew from financial positions, sold expensive homes, sold stocks, and made other moves to reduce exposure to losses. When the financial markets collapsed, those people did not suffer big losses. Some took positive action and reinvested in low-priced assets and experienced gains as the market returned toward normal.

Anticipating change is valuable in understanding the future. Anticipation allows you to avoid surprises in your life, or at least reduce the number of high-impact surprises. Anticipation allows you to prepare for the future.

STEEP

In an earlier chapter, I mentioned the categories of forces that many futurists follow:

- Social change
- Technological change
- Economic change
- Ecological change
- Political change

These are often referred to as the "STEEP" categories, using the first letter of each category to represent the group. These categories are usually thought of in terms of big change (in the world or a country), but they apply all the way down to your community and your neighborhood, so you should be aware of these changes and how, or if, they will impact you.

Social change may be on a global or very local scale. A country emerging from poverty, a growing religious movement, protest movements, revolution, immigration, increased education, and equality for minorities are all examples. The Internet has changed the way the world communicates. In your own community, you may see social change as schools teach children the language of their new country, as you communicate with friends around the world whom you have never met, or as your community changes zoning regulations, thereby impacting property owners. Somewhere between social change and technological change lies a generation of people born since 1990 that are digital natives. They have grown up with digital beeps, digital clocks, calculators, cell phones, computers, and all the other digital devices that are normal in our world today.

Technological change may be the most obvious area of change as you watch the continuing evolution of the Internet, new medical advances, space exploration, telephones that are becoming computers, robots (and your car) as they become smarter, and research that advances many fields rapidly. The technology in your own home is probably changing to make you more aware of the world around you, providing information about nearly everything. Your doctor has rapidly improving diagnostic tools; your community has increased surveillance tools to deter crime, and you can call people around the world free on your computer with live video.

Economic change on a large scale may come in many forms, including gradual inflation or a crushing recession. At a local level, governments may borrow money to build facilities or improve the local image but may raise your taxes to pay off the debt. In your community, a change in zoning, a new school, or an improved street may increase the value of your property but increase your taxes.

Ecologic change in the form of global warming is a serious concern world-wide, but ecology starts with individuals, homes, and communities. If your community allows a local industry to put pollution into the air or into local waters, that pollution not only contributes to the worldwide problems but may harm you or your family as well. Awareness or participation in local activities that reduce pollution or protect and restore the environment may have an impact on your life.

Political change is everywhere and constant, even when it is not apparent. Change is most obvious in countries and organizations that have open elections but continues even in countries that attempt to stifle change. In your community, understanding the political process and how it works can be very useful. Many communities have long-term, written plans in place, including plans to change or improve roads, annex adjacent properties, expand water and sewer systems, improve police and fire protection, and advance many other services. If you make the effort to learn what plans are pending or already in place, you will be better prepared to deal with their impacts.

SCANNING YOUR HORIZONS

Futurists use a method called environment scanning, or horizon scanning, which amounts to a conscious effort to watch for and be aware of change, which is why the STEEP categories were created. Scanning is a very useful tool that alerts businesses and organizations to any change that may have some impact. This tool can help you in your personal life as well.

	World	National	Local
Social	Millennials entering adult society	U.S./Mexico wall rising	U of Houston offers all Futures classes online.
Technology	Solar tech near competing with coal	Nanoscale research changing medicine	Surveillance increases
Economic	G-20 promises economic reform	Stock market rises Unemployment rising	Unemployment high
Ecologic	Ice caps shrinking Glaciers move faster	Electric cars in 2010 Hydrogen on horizon	
Political	Group of 20 replaces G-8	United States changing health care system	Real estate reform on Texas ballot

Figure 6.1 - A table for recording scanning results including some 2009 sample entries. You may wish to include the source and date for each entry.

Above is an example of a simple layout that you can create on your computer or on any sheet of paper to keep track of information you learn that may impact your future. The advantage of creating a table in your word processing software is that each section is expandable. You may find information in newspapers, magazines, television, online newsgroups, or almost anywhere. Scanning is simply a matter of paying attention, always asking yourself how any piece of information might impact you, your career, or your family in the future. One source for information on global trends is the Millennium Project Web site at http://www.millennium-project.org. The section titled "15 Global Challenges" is updated annually by futurists from all parts of the world.

The news media is very aware of scanning and trends, so you will see frequent articles or stories in the news about new trends that are changing the future. Read, look, and listen; then make up your own mind about what is really happening. You can get different viewpoints about nearly any potential trend on Google or your favorite search engine. As you read or listen, keep asking how this trend might affect you. Will your life change in some way? Will your children's lives be changed? When someone tells you about impending change, dig deeper. Remember how you made your own personal trend lines, and ask yourself, "What is causing this change?" Is there data, or is this someone's opinion? And keep asking, "Why? What is causing this trend line to move up or down?"

Just as your six personal domains help you understand what is changing in your personal world, the STEEP categories can help you understand what is happening in the world around you. So far, you have been collecting information about you and your world. After just a little more information, you will start using everything that you have learned about your life to start building your future.

EVERYTHING IS CONNECTED!

One of the difficulties with anticipating the future is that nearly everything is related to everything else, so when one element of society, or of your life, changes, other parts may change as well. So as you explore change in the world around you, consider how trends in one category might impact other categories.

For example, if prices of basic household commodities such as flour, soap, beans, and spices rise in a developing country, the people with the least money are likely to be affected the most.

Figure 6.2 - The economic category is related to the social category.

So the economy has changed, becoming more expensive. How will that affect subsistence farmers and others with little cash? Suppose, to earn more income, the farmers start cutting down trees to sell the logs for lumber and the limbs for firewood. That will give the farmers cash and more land to farm. However, logging inflicts damage to the ecosystem, removing habitat for animals, removing oxygen generators (trees), and disturbing the soil. In addition, the logs have to be transported by roads or waterways, inflicting additional impacts.

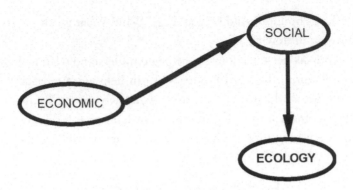

Figure 6.3 - The economic category is related to the social,
which is related to ecology.

The farmers are now seeing the economic benefits of selling logs and fire-wood, so they invest in new (for them) technology, chain saws, and eventually tractors.

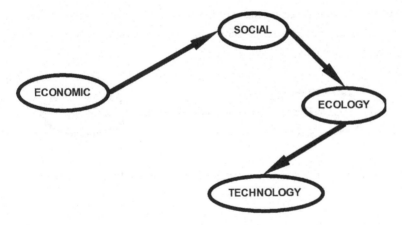

Figure 6.4 - Add technology!

The impacts of the logging now attract the attention of ecologists in other parts of the world who raise the alarm about the bad things that can happen as a result of this trend. Enter the politicians! They now have a constituency (farmers, truck drivers, chainsaw importers and others) who can vote!

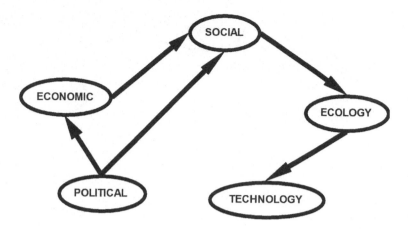

Figure 6.5 - Adding the political category completes the STEEP group.

Very quickly, we have involved all five of the STEEP categories, creating trends in each.

The same thing is true in your personal domains. A change in one domain will probably affect other domains. Below is a very simple relationship diagram showing your six personal domains, with no relationships shown yet.

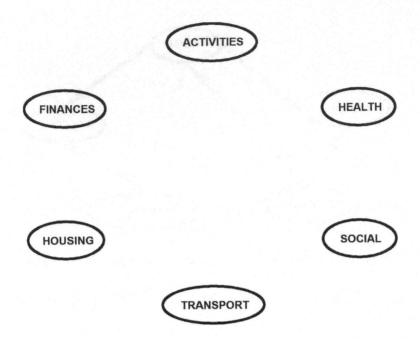

Figure 6.6 - A blank relationship diagram of personal domains.

Now, add some lines, starting with your career. Obviously, your career affects the finances domain. That is the reason people work! Your career will also directly impact the transportation domain, which in turn affects the finance domain. Your career also directly impacts your family, because time at work is time away from the family. Coworkers and business contacts are also an important part of the social domain.

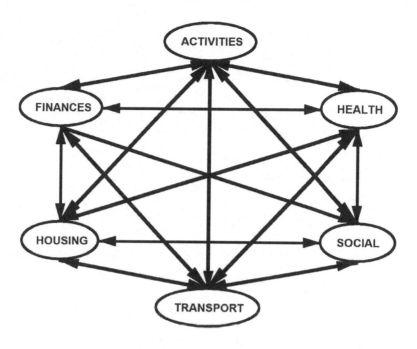

Figure 6.7 - Relationship diagram showing some
relationships between domains.

Arguments could be made that your career affects the health and housing domains, and this is true in some cases, but the diagram as we have it is true in most cases.

One more example, based on the health domain, which impacts each of the other domains directly:

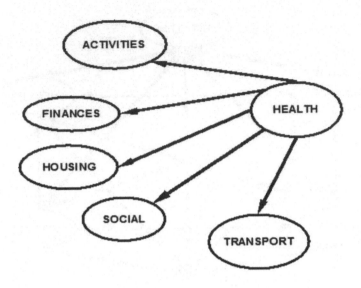

Figure 6.8 - The health domain impacts all other domains.

The health domain directly affects every other domain. As long as you have *good* health, all of the domains are impacted in a positive way. However, health and illness cost money in insurance and medical bills. Health also affects one's ability to work or to participate in sports, travel, and other activities. Health can affect the housing domain, determining the location and type of housing for those who are unable to care completely for themselves. The social domain is obviously affected by health, particularly when friends and family members provide care. Finally, the transportation domain is impacted by one's health. Vision, reactions, and hearing affect one's ability to drive a car, and public transportation or the kindness of friends are the only options for many.

You can create a relationship diagram with a pencil and paper for yourself or for anyone in your family. That will help you to see impacts and options that may be in your future.

In the next chapter, you will explore events that may occur in your life simply because similar events have occurred to other people in the same stage of life. You will be learning about your future from people who have already lived it!

CHAPTER 7

Events That Will Change Your Life

CONCEPT

MANY events occur during the course of each individual's life. Some will be positive, some negative, and some neutral. Many events can be anticipated, whether because they are common in most people's lives, or because they are the result of individual actions or behaviors. Events also vary in degree of impact, so it makes sense to focus on the events that will have the greatest impacts on your life.

Things happen in our lives. Good things, bad things; expected and unexpected; accidental and intentional. These are the personal events that occur throughout our lives. Some are probable, many plausible, all possible.

Earlier, in chapter 2, you saw that a simple timeline of life goes from birth to death.

In the next step, the timeline was divided into segments, or life stages. Finally, in chapter 3, the timeline was sliced along its length, dividing it into six domains. Each domain includes the ten life stages, and each life stage contains the six domains.

	Infant	Child	Adol-escent	Young Adult	Adult	Mid Age	Inde-pendent	Vulner-able	Depend-ent	End Life
Activities										
Finance										
Health										
Housing										
Social										
Transport										

Figure 7.1 - The timeline is expanded to include the six personal domains in each life stage. This is the format for many of the worksheets that will follow.

In this chapter, you are going to explore plausible events in your life and add them to your personal timeline. The important thing to understand about life events is that each event occurs in one stage on your timeline and in one domain.

The importance of that bit of information is that you can anticipate some events because you know *about* when they are likely to occur in your timeline. Some events are directly related to a life stage and are nearly certain to occur during that stage (puberty occurs during adolescence, menopause during middle age, for example). Other events have a higher probability in one stage than another (accidental injuries are common during adolescence and young adult stages; retirement usually occurs during the independent stage), and other events can happen at any time.

Bracketing is a simple technique that can help you anticipate some events that may be in your future. You put brackets around an event by identifying the earliest date and the latest date the event could occur, so the event should happen sometime between those dates. As you get nearer to the anticipated event, you may be able to narrow the time range and see clues as to when the event will happen.

For example, I live near the Gulf Coast of Texas, so we have to be concerned about hurricanes each year. The annual hurricane season starts in June and ends in November. Those are my big brackets, but experience tells me that the greatest concern will be in July through September, the smaller brackets. Once the hurricane season starts, I pay attention to the weather reports of tropical storms forming in the Atlantic and moving toward the Gulf. If a storm enters the Gulf, I pay more attention to the forecasts of the storm's path. If the storm develops as a hurricane and keeps moving in our direction, I start making preparations to secure our home and to leave the area.

The same approach works with many life events, even those that seem far away. Retirement is an event that may be far off in your future, but you know that it will come in some form, probably during your sixties or seventies. If you start thinking about your retirement now—about what you would like that retirement to be—you can take steps in each of your domains over the years ahead to assure that you will be prepared when the event arrives.

TYPES OF EVENTS

There are several categories of events that have implications for your future, and some events may be in more than one category.

Turning point events change the direction of your life. Marriage, becoming a parent, divorce, choosing a trade or career, immigration, dropping out of school, loss of health, and death of a spouse are examples. Each of these events will not only cause your life to be different from what it was (often very quickly) but will also change the nature of future events.

Life cycle or biological events include growing, developing, aging, and death. These events are very closely related to life stages, so they can be anticipated with some accuracy and should not present many surprises in your life.

Legal events are events that are based on laws or legislation. Often these are events that relate to eligibility based on age, such as when a child is old enough for school, a teen is eligible for a driver's license, old enough to vote, or eligible for military service, and when workers become eligible for health care and retirement benefits. Some events are the result of breaking laws and result in fines, jail, or prison terms. Other events such as forming a business or buying a home have many legal requirements, including documents and tax payments. Many of these events are also predictable, and they will be part of your future.

Intentional or choice events. Most of the turning-point events are the result of intention or choice, but people make smaller decisions and choices every day. Many of those choices have impacts on our lives. Some example are: decisions about education, use of credit or debt, investments, choice of neighborhoods, diet, exercise, and general health habits. Those may each be small decisions at the time they are made, but they may lead to sizable impacts, positive or negative, later in life. Sometimes you will make deliberate decisions to change something in your life or set goals for something that you want to achieve.

Unintentional events are those over which you have little or no control, where actions, situations, or decisions are by others. These events would include accidents, decisions by family members or friends, natural disasters, and layoffs.

Wild card events. "Wild card" is a term used by futurists to describe an event that has a high impact if it occurs but has a low probability of occurring. The following paragraphs will discuss impacts and probabilities in more detail, but examples of wild cards include winning the lottery, learning that the baby you are expecting will actually be quintuplets, or being struck by lightning.

Events by Stages

Below is a table of common events in life and the life stages in which those events are likely to occur. This listing is intended to give you *some* indication of events to anticipate or prepare for at different times of life. For the most part, these events are common in the U.S. middle class, but not everywhere. Some events, first births for example, are affected by cultural patterns and socio-economic status.

Examples of common and high-impact life events

Life Stage	Common	High impact
Infant	Learning, walking, talking Minor illnesses	Serious illness
Child	Growth Minor injuries and illnesses	Serious illness Bullying Parents divorce
Adolescent	School Puberty, emotions, sex Growth Begin driving Risky behaviors	Accidents, serious injuries Arrest Pregnancy Parents divorce Death of parent or friend
Young adult	Complete education Begin career Move out of parents' home Marriage First child	Accidents Illness or injury of child Job loss or change Divorce

Adult	Career pressures or advances Managing family Last child	Financial problems Divorce Job loss
Middle age	Menopause, end child bearing Aging signs Empty nest Grandchildren Parents retire Peak earnings, savings	Serious or chronic illness, self or spouse. Parent illness or death Crime victim Job loss Divorce
Independent elder	Eligible for retirement Social Security, Medicare Work/retirement choices Discretionary time Increased aging signs Relocate, new friends Travel Problems in children's lives	Retirement Changing roles and social life Serious illness, self or spouse Death of spouse Become caregiver Stop driving Victim of crime
Vulnerable elder	Frailty Cognitive problems Risk of falls Risk of scams	Falls, injuries Assisted living Victim of crime
Dependent elder	Reduced activities Increased medical care	Dependent on others Losing control of life Nursing home
End of life	Greatly reduced activities Increased medical, "Good-byes"	Terminal diagnosis Hospice

Figure 7.2 - Some common and high-impact life events
for each stage of life.

IMPACTS OF EVENTS ON YOUR LIFE

Some events will have powerful impacts on your life, yet others will have little impact at all. For example, the birth of a child, a heart attack, or retirement are each high-impact events.

How do you recognize or define impacts? Are there different types? Following are a few examples:

Shock/grief: Some high-impact negative events can cause shock, grief, or both. The death of a child or a spouse could cause both.

Elation/relief: High-impact, positive events can bring feelings of elation or relief. Winning the lottery would obviously bring elation. Learning that mother and child are both doing well after a birth would probably bring both elation and relief.

Change: Many events bring about change. Whether the change is large or small, it may impact your future. Getting married, starting a new job, or having children all create change in your life.

Fear: Some events cause fear. Violence, serious illness in yourself or a stakeholder, or the death of a spouse may all cause fear—either about the present or about the future.

Some interesting research into life events actually ranks the impacts of various life events. The research ranks individual events, such as divorce or going to jail, from highest to lowest impact. In these cases, the impact of the original event may be similar for many people, but for others, the aftershocks go on long after the event. For some, the initial event may be the start of a descent into long-term misery. Going to jail may be as simple as a few days or a month in jail, then it is over. For others, going to jail may be years or decades in prison, with very little opportunity to return to a normal life once released. Being fired from work can be devastating, but the long-term impact of months of unemployment and uncertainty can be even more stressful.

On the other hand, positive events can also have continuing long-term impacts. A marriage may get better every year. A promotion may lead to many positive, continuing events. The birth of a child is just the start of a chain of events that can provide continuing change throughout your life.

The following list of events is from a list created by researchers Thomas

Holmes and Richard Rahe in 1967, then modified and extended in 1995 by
Mark Miller and Richard Rahe. The researchers had noticed that people often
experienced diseases or conditions following stressful life events, so they set
out to identify life-changing events and their impacts. Our approach here is
the reverse of that research in that you will become aware of the potential stress
related to these events in advance and be prepared to deal with them before
they happen.

Most people do not have that advantage; once the event has occurred,
they are in such a stressful situation that they do not know how to cope with
the event or the aftermath. Here is the list, starting with the most stressful or
life-changing events down to the least stressful.

1. Death of a child
2. Death of a spouse
3. Death of a sibling
4. Death of a parent
5. Divorce
6. Death of a family member
7. Fired from work
8. Separation from spouse
9. Major injury or illness
10. Separation or marital problems
11. Jail term
12. Pregnancy
13. Miscarriage or abortion
14. Death of a close friend
15. Adoption of child
16. Birth of child
17. Business readjustment
18. Decreased income
19. Parents' divorce
20. Relative moving in
21. Investment/credit problems
22. Foreclosure
23. Marital reconciliation
24. Health change family member

25. Gain of family member
26. Change in financial state
27. Change in arguments
28. Retirement
29. Major decision (re future)
30 Accident
31. Separation due to work
32. Remarriage of a parent
33. Move (different town)
34. Change to different work
35. Falling out of a relationship
36. Marriage
37. Spouse changes work
38. Birth of a grandchild
39. Child leaves home (other)
40. Property loss or damage
41. Engagement to marry
42. Moderate injury or illness
43. Mortgage, more than $10,000
44. Child leaves home (marriage)
45. Child leaves home (college)
46. Change in living conditions
47. Sexual difficulties
48. Demotion at work
49. Increased income
50. Change work responsibilities
51. Relationship problems
52. Change in residence
53. Trouble with in-laws
54. Major purchase
55. Begin/end school or college
56. New relationship
57. Outstanding achievement
58. Trouble with coworkers
59. Change in schools
60. Change in work hours

61. Trouble with supervisors
62. Transfer at work
63. Promotion at work
64. Change in religious beliefs
65. Christmas
66. More work responsibilities
67. Change in eating habits
68. Trouble with the boss
69. Mortgage less than $10,000
70. Work troubles (other)
71. Change in recreation
72. Change in social activities
73. Change in sleep
74. Change in get-togethers
75. Change in personal habits
76. Move (within same town)
77. Major dental work
78. Vacation
79.Change in political beliefs
80. A minor injury or illness
81. Moderate purchase.
82. Fewer responsibilities at work
83. Change in church activities
84. Minor violation of law
85. Correspondence course

Each of these events can have different meanings and different impacts for any individual. Men and women will react differently to some situations, and events may have a greater impact at one age or stage of life than in another.

Again, the reason for this long list of events is to give you the opportunity to consider each event and whether that event may occur in your life. Now, long before the event occurs is the time to ask yourself, "If or when this event occurs, how will I deal with it?" Anticipation of future events is a way to reduce the number of surprises in your life, particularly the negative surprises.

Probabilities

What is the probability of any event happening, and which events are important?

The list of events above includes a lot of high-impact events, and some of those events may happen to you over the next ten years. Take a few minutes to go back over the list. For each event in the list, assign a rating for the next ten years using a scale of one (not at all likely) to five (will almost certainly happen). This will get you started thinking about probabilities and possibilities, and will provide you with lists of events that you will need in later chapters.

Not all high-probability events will be important as you plan for the future. Impact is usually more important. For example, your next birthday is a high-probability event, but it is not very useful in planning for your future. Birthdays and anniversaries are examples of high-probability events that generally do not have much impact on your life

A Favorite Tool of Futurists

Very simple, yet very effective, the two-axis matrix is helpful in determining the importance of events to your future. This is something you can do anywhere—on a pad of paper, a napkin, or your computer. You can plot a single event or many events in one diagram, which is based on two simple scales. In our example, the scales will be Impact and Probability. Assuming this is your first experience with a two-axis matrix, here is how it works:

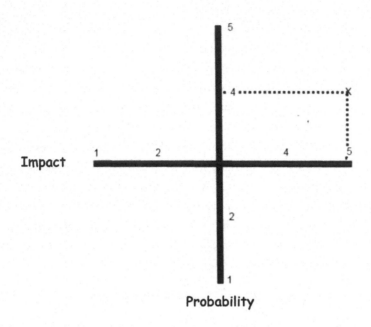

Figure 7.3 - Rate any event on both scales: probability and impact. The event above is marked (X) as a probability of 4 and an impact of 5. The four spaces created by the intersecting lines are quadrants.

In order to put several events into one diagram, just make a numbered list of events that you think might occur in the next ten years, then enter each number into the two-axis matrix. For example, if you are now twenty years old, your list might include:

1. Complete schooling/training
2. Start work/career
3. Marriage
4. First child
5. First home
6. Health problem
7. Weight gain
8. Divorce

9. School reunion
10. Parking ticket

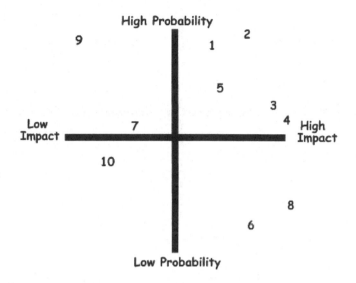

Figure 7.4 - Ten events over the next ten years are shown in the four quadrants of a two-axis matrix.

Notice the number of events (1, 2, 3, 4, 5) in the upper-right quadrant, which combines high probability with high impact. These are events that will have a strong impact, and will probably occur. Consequently, you should not only be prepared for these events to happen but should develop strategies and a plan for dealing with each of them.

The events in the lower-right quadrant (6, 8) also have a high impact but are not likely to happen. Yet, you should be aware of these possibilities and be prepared to deal with them if they do occur. In the upper-left quadrant are events (7, 9) that will probably happen, but will not have much impact. In the lower-left quadrant are the events (10) that probably will not happen and would not have much impact on your life if they did.

Now that you see how to put plausible future events into a matrix, you may be wondering why you are going through this exercise. The next diagram will help explain. Each sector or quadrant in the matrix indicates the type of planning for the future for that quadrant.

Figure 7.5 - This matrix suggests your planning needs for events in each quadrant.

This is a diagram to remember. It identifies how you should deal with future events in each of the four quadrants.

Routine Planning. This quadrant is for events you put on your calendar or planner such as birthdays, anniversaries, appointments, happenings, and meetings.

Strategic Planning. In this quadrant, you will have high-impact, high-probability events. You will need to prepare for these events, developing strategies and plans so that you have a clear idea of how you are going to deal with each.

Contingency Planning. This is the area for wild cards and high-impact, low-probability events. For each personal event, you should consider a contingency plan to have in place in case the event occurs.

Planning Not Necessary. The heading says it all. There is no need to make plans for events that are unlikely to occur and that have little or no impact if they do occur.

The rest of the pages in this chapter are lists of common events, arranged by life stage in order to help you anticipate events for the next ten years of your life; they provide a reference for your future life stages.

You will see this diagram (7.5) again in the strategic-planning section.

Events by Life Stage

On this and the following pages are tables for each life stage, with *some* events that may occur during that stage. Socioeconomic status will affect some of these events or their probability of occurrence in a stage.

Life stage—Infant

Personal domains—forces in life	Common or typical events in this stage	Positive events	Negative events	Wild card events
Activities	Motor skills develop Learning First words First steps	Learning		
Finances	Provided by parents		High-expense illness Family poverty	
Health	Growth Development Childhood illnesses	Healthy	Malnutrition Inadequate care Serious injury	
Housing	Parent's home			
Social	Parents, siblings		Parents divorce Abuse	Death of parent
Transportation	Provided by parents			

Figure 7.6 - Some events that may occur during the infant stage of life.

Life stage—Child

Personal domains—forces in life	Common or typical events in this stage	Positive events	Negative events	Wild card events
Activities	Start school Sports, games, school activities Pet(s)	Achievement Safe school	Failure	Extreme achievement
Finances	Provided by parents		Family poverty High-expense illness	
Health	Physical growth Cognitive development Contagious childhood diseases Minor injuries	Healthy	Poor nutrition Inadequate care Serious injury or illness	Disability
Housing	Parent's home	Safe home Safe neighborhood	Unsafe neighborhood	
Social	Social development Birth of sibling Schoolmates Day care Both parents working Change of schools	Good relationships and friendships	Parents divorce Abuse Bullying Home alone Death of grandparent	Death of parent
Transportation	Provided by parents School bus			

Figure 7.7 - Some events that may occur during the child stage of life.

Life stage—Adolescent

Personal domains— forces in life	Common or typical events in this stage	Positive events	Negative events	Wild card events
Activities	Secondary school Complete public school Prepare for higher education Competitive sports Start trade school or university First job(s)	Success Achievements Graduation Good school	Unsafe school Crime Failure Dropout	Arrest Scholarship
Finances	First earnings First money management		High-expense illness Family poverty	
Health	Puberty Growth spurts, strength Strong emotions First sexual encounter	Healthy	Alcohol, drugs, tobacco Serious injury Pregnancy Sexual disease Depression	Suicide Homicide victim Rehabilitation Birth of child Career athlete
Housing	Parent's home First housing away from parent's home	Safe neighborhood	Unsafe neighborhood	
Social	First romance First breakup Asserting independence, identity Risky behaviors Illness or death of grandparent	Respect for parents Trust in family	Parents divorce Abuse Bullying Gang	Death of parent Death of a friend
Transportation	Independent use public transport Learn to drive Driver's license First car		Traffic ticket Auto accident	

Figure 7.8 - Some events that may occur during the adolescent stage of life.

Note that "Death of a parent" is listed as a wild card event for the first three stages of life, but not in succeeding stages. Wild card events are described as events with a low probability of occurring, but if they do occur, they have a strong impact on the individual. In later stages of life, the death of a parent becomes more plausible and generally has less impact. On the other hand, divorce may be a high-impact event for children and teenagers, but it is not considered a low-probability event in those stages.

Life stage—Young Adult

Personal domains—forces in life	Common or typical events in this stage	Positive events	Negative events	Wild card events
Activities	Complete education Begin trade or career Active in sports	Achievements Advancement	Failure(s) Fired or jobless	Extreme success
Finances	Responsible for personal and family finances	Successful management of affairs	Financial problems	
Health	Physical maturity Brain achieves full growth	Good health	Health problems Alcohol or drug problems Injury or accident	Homicide victim
Housing	Responsible for housing, self, and family. Select region, community, home	Good, happy home	Inadequate housing Declining neighborhood	Major relocation
Social	Independent: responsible for self and family or partner Marriage or cohabitation Parenthood, children	Fall in love Develop new social circles	Partner violence Divorce Crime victim	Suicide of family member Multiple birth— twins, triplets, or more
Transportation	Provide or arrange family transportation Commute	International travel	Accident	Public transport accident

Figure 7.9 - Some events that may occur
during the young adult stage of life.

Life stage—Adult

Personal domains— forces in life	Common or typical events in this stage	Positive events	Negative events	Wild card events
Activities	Career advancement Career pressures Sports with children	Recognition Promotion	Fired or jobless	Major advancement
Finances	Financial pressures New mortgage	Increasing income	Inadequate income	Extreme success
Health	Past peak health May neglect health Weight gain	Fitness	Health problems	
Housing	Larger home	Good neighborhood	Declining neighborhood	Foreclosure
Social	Teenagers becoming independent Multiple time demands Marriage or cohabitation		Divorce Injury or illness of child	Death of child or spouse
Transportation	Transporting children	Easy commute	Auto accident Excessive travel	

Figure 7.10 - Some events that may occur during the adult stage of life.

Life stage—Middle Age

Personal domains—forces in life	Common or typical events in this stage	Positive events	Negative events	Wild card events
Activities	Career peak	Expertise valued Scale back on work	Jobless	Start second career
Finances	Income peak Increased assets Retirement saving	Financially fit Pay off mortgage	Financial problems	Major income or asset change
Health	Menopause, end child bearing Vision changes (bifocals) Wrinkles, sags, gray Health problems and risks	Physically fit	Heart attack, stroke, cancer, diabetes, depression	Triathlon!
Housing	Nest is emptying	Second home	Lose home	
Social	Adult children— marriages Grandchildren born Divorce risk	Achievements Recognition	Parent illness or death Adult children at home Divorce	Parenting grandchildren
Transportation			Auto accident	

Figure 7.11 - Some events that may occur during the
middle age stage of life.

In the midlife stage, at about age fifty, one's parents are generally in their seventies or older and may need help or require care. At the same time, many adult children—recent college graduates or newly divorced—move back home to live with parents before going out on their own. This phenomenon has created the term "sandwich generation" for people in midlife who are helping both their parents and their grown children. People in middle age may also find themselves raising grandchildren.

Life stage—Independent Elder

Personal domains— forces in life	Common or typical events in this stage	Positive events	Negative events	Wild card events
Activities	Eligible for retirement Discretionary time Travel and leisure activities Stop working	Second career Volunteer Continuing education	Loss of role(s)	New career
Finances	Social security Government health insurance Fixed income Will, living will, instructions to physicians	Adequate income and assets No mortgage No debt	Inadequate savings Financial problems Reduced income	
Health	Chronic conditions and multiple medications Skin loses elasticity, age spots, white hair, shorter, vision problems, aches, and pains.	Physically fit Regular exercise	Health problems Heart attack, stroke, cancer, diabetes, etc Frailty Decline of vision, hearing, or mobility	Extreme long life
Housing	Relocate Downsize	New home	Inadequate housing or neighborhood	Loss of home
Social	Great Grandchildren Change of social circles Spouse illness Living alone	New friends Adult grandchildren Involvement with people and life	Caregiver to spouse Death of spouse Problems in child's family Abuse, scams	Birth of child
Transportation	Reduced transport needs Declining driving skills		Accident Lose driving privileges Inadequate transportation	Self-driving cars available!

Figure 7.12 - Some events that may occur during the independent elder stage of life.

Life stage—Vulnerable Elder

Personal domains—forces in life	Common or typical events in this stage	Positive events	Negative events	Wild card events
Activities	Reduced activities More passive activities	Able to participate in activities	Unable to participate	
Finances	Limited ability to manage finances	Adequate income and assets	Poverty	
Health	Difficulty with IADLs * Physically or mentally vulnerable to becoming dependent Frailty Cognitive problems	Generally healthy	Risk of falls Dementia Alzheimer's diagnosis	Suicide Return to independent stage
Housing	Home, with spouse or help Assisted living	At home	Nursing home	
Social	Reliant on family, friends, or caregiver	Supportive family Enjoying life	Abuse or neglect Scams Crime victim	
Transportation	Reliant on others for transport	Transport is provided	Transport is not available	

Figure 7.13 - Some events that may occur during the vulnerable elder stage of life.

*IADLs are the instrumental activities of daily living, and include using the telephone, shopping, using transportation, preparing meals, housecleaning, taking medications, and managing money.

Life stage—Dependent Elder

Personal domains— forces in life	Common or typical events in this stage	Positive events	Negative events	Wild card events
Activities	Limited to passive activities.	Able to participate with others	Unable to participate	
Finances	Reduced ability to handle financial affairs	Able to manage finances	Unable to manage personal affairs Pressures from family members	
Health	Difficulty with several activities of daily living (ADLs)* Require long-term care Multiple medications Pressure sores Pneumonia	Good health despite disability	Excessive medication Emergency room	Recovery to independent stage Suicide
Housing	At-home care Nursing home or assisted living	At home or home-like atmosphere		
Social	Limited ability to meet with or communicate with people	Phone calls, emails, letters, and visits with family and friends Enjoying life	Difficult or limited access to phone or other means of communication Abuse or neglect	
Transportation	Provided by others. May be limited to special vehicles or ambulance	Travel	Unable to get out of residence easily.	

Figure 7.14 - Some events that may occur
during the dependent elder stage of life.

ADLs are the physical activities of daily living—bathing, dressing, personal grooming, toileting, continence, and transferring.

Life stage—End of Life

Personal domains—forces in life	Common or typical events in this stage	Positive events	Negative events	Wild card events
Activities	Very limited activities Instructions and arrangements for death	Family events	Isolation	
Finances	Complete financial affairs and arrangements			
Health	Terminal diagnosis Second opinion Denial, anger, bargaining, depression, acceptance Palliative care, hospice care	Acceptance Receive care from family and professionals Avoid pain or discomfort	Discomfort or pain Emergency room	Return to independent stage Suicide or assisted suicide
Housing	Home Nursing home Hospice facility			
Social	Good-byes to family and friends	Time with friends, family	Friends, family withdraw Family disputes Family refusal to let go	
Transportation	Dependent on others Limited needs			

Figure 7.15 - Some events that may occur
during the end-of-life stage of life.

Note that recovery to the independent stage is listed as a wild card event in the dependent stage and the end-of-life stage. Some stroke victims in the dependent stage make unexpected recoveries, and some people diagnosed with terminal cancer also return to the independent stage.

The number of events shown in these profiles is obviously limited by space and an attempt to remain relatively universal. These profiles lean toward populations in developed countries.

In addition to the events listed here, a number of events are significant within different cultures, such as those celebrating the coming of age. These profiles are intended to remind you of possible events in your future, as well as events that may occur in the lives of your parents, your spouse, your children, grandchildren, and great grandchildren.

In the next chapter, you will identify and consider your personal values. Your values are your guides as you make decisions about your future.

CHAPTER 8

Personal Values: Your Guides to the Future

CONCEPT

EVERY individual and organization has values, even if they have not been stated. Your values are your beliefs, your personal rules, so they guide your behavior and your actions. They will also guide your way to the future.

What is *really* important to you? What do you value in your life? Love? Money? Respect? Power? In this chapter, you are going to be asked to think about your values—about what is really important to you.

Some values are set out for us by the laws of society, the commandments of religion, or even our parents' Golden Rule. The question is: what are the values that you pick for yourself? What do you think is right and wrong, good or bad? What are the values and ethics that are expected by your employer or your profession?

For the moment, assume that you accept and follow the rules of society, religion, and parents. That still leaves a lot of room for personal decisions about what is important to you.

PERSONAL VALUES

That is what this chapter is about: identifying and defining *your* values. It is also about helping you to prepare for those times in your future when your values conflict and you have to make choices. Understanding your values will not resolve all situations, but it will help you to anticipate conflicts and develop your own guidelines or strategies for dealing with them.

Values analysis examines what is important in your life. You probably know that you have values, and you probably know pretty much what those values are. However, have you ever written them down or compared them? Have you asked yourself which values are most important to you? Most people have beliefs about honesty, integrity, and the value of human life—but when push comes to shove, which values are most important in your mind? Values analysis will clarify your thinking in this area.

Why are personal values important to understanding your future? Because your values are, to quite an extent, the rudder of your life. Your values guide your actions, and your actions lead you to your future.

Think about that for a moment. Everyone has different values, which tends to lead us each to different futures. Some values are cultural, some are religious, and some are simply what most people learned as children.

- Thou shalt not kill
- Do not steal
- Help the weak, sick, and poor
- Obey the laws
- Tell the truth

There are many more examples of cultural and personal values, but you probably already see the point. Your personal values will drive many of your personal decisions, large and small. Some of those decisions will impact, or at least guide, your future.

In my workshops, I give people a short list of common values, and then I ask them to list those values in order of importance in their lives. There is a little more time and space here in this book, however, so you have a fairly long list of values (below) to pick from. Choose the values that are most important to you. Ten or twelve will give you a good starting point.

Advancement	Happiness	Power / Influence
Adventure	Health	Pride
Affection	Helping Others	Privacy
Achievement	Honesty	Professional Growth
Being best	Human Rights	Professional Relationships
Being liked	Humility	Quality Relationships
Career	Humor/Fun	Recognition
Challenge	Image	Relationships
Commitment	Improvement	Religion
Community Service	Income	Reputation
Compassion	Independence	Respect
Competence	Influence	Responsibility
Competition	Inner Harmony	Risk Taking
Continuous	Intellectual Status	Safety
Contribution to Others	Integrity	Security
Control	Involvement	Self Respect
Cooperation	Job Security	Self-Discipline
Creativity	Knowledge	Service To Others
Decisiveness	Leadership	Stability
Democracy	Learning	Status
Ecological Awareness	Leisure	Success
Economic Security	Long-term Perspective	Teamwork
Education	Looking good	Time Freedom
Environment	Loyalty	Work With Others
Ethics/Principles	Making a difference	Working Alone
Excellence	Money	Tradition
Excitement	Net Worth	Trust
Fairness	Performance	Truth
Fame	Perseverance	Vision
Family	Personal Development	Wealth
Financial Security	Personal Legacy/Estate	Wisdom
Freedom	Personal/Family Image	Work
Friends	Physical challenge	
Generosity	Pleasure	
Geographic Location	Pleasing others	
Growth	Politics	

Figure 8.1 - A list of personal values.

To this list of values, add any other personal values that are important to you. Next, mark or make a list of the values that are *most* important to you. Some of the items on the list sound nearly the same, so pick the one that seems best to you. Finally, rewrite your list, putting your values in order of importance. You will then have a list of what is most important in your life.

Which values are your top ten in order of importance?

For example, if your top three values are career, family, and wealth, which of those three is really number one? Throughout your life, you will have to make choices that will occasionally pit one value against another. Which value trumps another value? Family? Career? Wealth? Under what circumstances?

Wrestling with decisions about your values now will help you deal with many challenges that arise in your daily life. Dealing with these daily challenges based on your values provides a set of standards in your life that will help you make good decisions when the stakes are higher.

CAREER AND PROFESSIONAL VALUES

Now that you have decided what your personal values are, ask yourself which values are expected or required by your employer or your profession. Are they different from your personal values? Honesty is probably at the top of the list with most employers and professions, although family considerations may not be on their lists at all. Sometimes employers do not spell out their values, and you will have to learn their true values over time.

Professions usually have a code of ethics that sets out the values of the profession, promising honesty, fairness, and integrity or other values as a commitment to the people or organizations that rely on that profession.

DIFFERENCES AND CONFLICTS OF VALUES

Even when you know what your values are, you will sometimes have conflicts. You will have to pick one value over another.

A very simple example: Tomorrow is Saturday. The office is quiet, you have a big project coming up, and you could get a lot of work done on a quiet Saturday morning. That fits in with your work ethic value, but—your daughter has a soccer game in the morning and your son has a Little League game in the afternoon. They each feel that it is *very* important that you come to their game. What do you do?

You may find that you will have to reconcile or deal with conflicts between your personal values and the values of organizations or groups of which you are part. Examples could include schools, employers, your religion, a professional organization, or groups of friends.

Organizations will sometimes profess one set of values but practice a different set. Their products may not live up to the advertising, they may over-bill for professional services, or they may fail to meet deadlines. If you work for, represent, or do business with one of these organizations, how will those actions impact you, and how do you reconcile your values?

What if you and your spouse have conflicting values? You may find that differences in values are not really cause for conflict, but if you both want your own way about nearly everything, that is conflict. This book cannot tell you how to resolve problems of conflicting values, but it can help you recognize differences and make you aware of the potential for conflicts in the future.

The following diagrams illustrate some possible combinations of values between you and other individuals or organizations. The area of overlap is where you and someone else have common values. That can be a lot or a little. In the first illustration, there are no apparent common values.

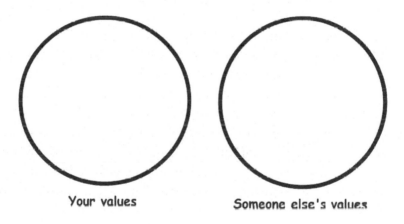

Your values   Someone else's values

Figure 8.2 - The values of two individuals are represented
by the circles, but their personal values are unknown.

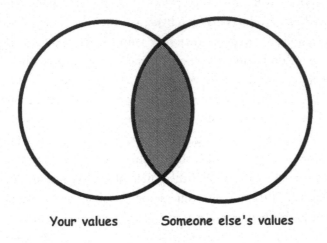

Your values   Someone else's values

Figure 8.3 - Two parties have some overlap in values.

Figure 8.3 might represent the relationship between individuals and organizations such as businesses in which there is some sharing of values, such as respect for commercial law and personal or property rights, but have very little else in common. This may also be the assumed overlap of values between students, coworkers, or other groups of people who do not really know each other well yet may meet each other frequently or even daily in person or online.

Some people, societies, or organizations may hold such strongly opposing values that they appear unable to find anything in common. How would you relate to someone with strongly held values that that are in opposition to your own?

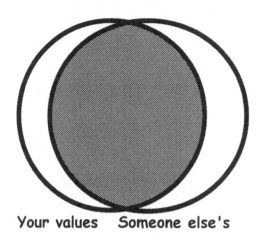

Your values   Someone else's

Figure 8.4 - A large overlap of values between two parties.

There is a large overlap in values between the two parties in figure 8.4, probably typical between friends and family members, or even within societies. This large overlap of values is more common than you might expect. In a society that respects laws and individual rights, the differences in values between members of that society may be small. Now that you have looked at your own values and the values of people and organizations around you, you should be better prepared to deal with some of the situations or conflicts that may arise in the future. More importantly, you now know more about your foundation of values.

Your values will be a good starting point in the next chapter, which is the final step in all this self-examination before you start developing scenarios about your future. Futurists call this analysis "SWOT" for strengths, weaknesses, opportunities, and threats. Your values will be one of your strengths.

CHAPTER 9

Realistically You: Strengths, Weaknesses, Opportunities, and Threats

CONCEPT

SWOT is an analytical tool that helps individuals or organizations analyze characteristics that will strongly influence change in the future. Analysis of each of the four SWOT areas starts preparing you to not only anticipate the future but to realistically prepare for and deal with future events. Also in this chapter is another tool, the futures wheel or mind map, which is very useful for linking ideas or brainstorming with others.

SWOT stands for strengths, weaknesses, opportunities, and threats. This is a tool that has been successfully used in corporate strategic planning for decades. Now you have an opportunity to see how effective this tool is when you scale it down to your personal life.

The traditional approach to SWOT analysis is to use a two-axis matrix, listing your strengths in one quadrant, weaknesses in another, and so on. This is a good system if you have given a lot of thought to each of the four categories, but most of us need a little more to go on. If you are asked for a list of your strengths, your first thought may be, "Strengths in what?"

Starting with a blank page does not do much to stimulate thinking, so we are going to take a more direct approach that will give you more clues and more to think about. First, think of strengths and weaknesses as internal concerns, strictly personal. Next, think of opportunities and threats as external concerns from the world around you.

Strengths and Weaknesses

Start with your strengths and weaknesses, and look at them in *each* of your six domains. Figure 9.1 shows some examples of both strengths and weaknesses that a person might recognize in each personal domain.

In each of these tables are listed only a few fictitious examples to help get you started.

Internal Factors	My Strengths (Knowledge, abilities, skills, experience)	My Weaknesses (Knowledge, abilities, skills)
Activities (School, career, sports, religion)	Good education, training, experience. Athletic Write, speak, computer	Math skills Artistic English only
Finance	Good income Good credit history Adequate insurance	Big mortgage Credit card debt High taxes Inadequate retirement fund
Health	Excellent health Good physical condition	Getting older Family history of cancer
Housing	Good home Good neighborhood	Big mortgage High maintenance
Social	Close, supportive family Good appearance, social skills Very good references	Not good networker Not socially aggressive
Transport (Mobility)	Two reliable cars Short commute	Inadequate public transport Fear of flying

Figure 9.1 - Examples of one individual's strengths and weaknesses.

When you divide the question about your strengths into the six personal domains the answers become very specific and are no longer vague or complex. Keep in mind that it is okay to break any domain down into smaller parts.

The activities domain includes everything that you do—school, career, religion, sports, hobbies, travel, etc. You may have strengths in any of these areas. For example, speaking a second or third language is a personal strength when traveling. Language skills can also be a strength in your career. If you have been elected to office in *any* organization, that position reflects leadership and responsibility, which are important strengths.

The point is that you should look carefully at all of your strengths and recognize them for what they are.

Now comes the hard part: recognizing your weaknesses. Part of the value of doing this is that once you recognize a weakness, you can do something about it. Many of us choose careers that avoid our weaknesses and rely on our strengths. Some people have trouble with math and science, while others cannot work comfortably with other people. Many people cannot draw well, many are afraid to speak to groups of people, and others are afraid of flying in airplanes.

Some of these weaknesses will affect your choices of careers, and others will affect the career you are already in. Acknowledging and recognizing your weaknesses will help you deal with or even overcome them in the future.

This process for analyzing your strengths and weaknesses continues through all six domains, giving you a well-rounded picture of all aspects of your life. This analysis also has the benefit of drawing your attention to what you need to change and identifying the strengths you can put to use.

Next, you will explore the external factors in your life: opportunities and threats. Again, you will break these categories down into the major driving forces in the world around you, the STEEP categories we explored in chapter 6. You will also look at opportunities and threats geographically, as shown in figures 9.2 and 9.3.

OPPORTUNITIES

Notice that the columns encourage you to think about each of the categories on a global, national, and local basis. Global and national forces will often appear to be vague or distant and out of your control, while local forces are likely to have the most direct impact on your life.

External Opportunities	Global	National	Local
Social	Improving healthcare worldwide Slowing population growth	Rising employment	Community involvement
Technology	Easy communication Availability of knowledge Increasing availability of solar and wind power	Nanotech/medical Stem cell medicine Preventive medicine	Home power (solar, wind) generation Preventive medicine
Economy	International growth in markets Greater global interdependence	Economic growth Increasing employment	Home value rising Investment opportunities
Ecology	Awareness of ecological balance	Efforts to reduce impacts on planet	Improved water and drainage systems
Politics	Reduction of conflicts	Increasing transparency Increasing access to info	Increasing awareness of public and voters

Figure 9.2 - A few examples of external opportunities.

Starting with opportunities, what are the opportunities that you see in each STEEP category and in each of the three geographic areas over the next ten years? At first you might wonder about the opportunities in global change, but in looking at major trends or changes in the world you may also find that they may cause impacts on your life. A growing global economy may improve your employment or career opportunities. Reduced political tensions and conflicts also increase other opportunities, whether for business or for personal travel.

When you bring the forces of change down to the local level, it is easier to see the direct impacts on your life. If your local hospital installs a high-resolution CT imaging system and then offers early warning cancer screening, that can impact your life. If your community improves streets, lighting, or drainage in your neighborhood, that could increase the value of your home and improve the quality of your life.

Improving the quality of your life in the future is what this exercise is all about. Thinking seriously about your future is the best way to improve your future quality of life.

THREATS

Now for the threats. What do you see in the world, your country, or your community that threatens your future over the next ten years or longer?

External Threats	Global	National	Local
Social	Wars Hunger, underemployment	Flu Drugs and addiction	Immigration Gang problems Unemployment
Technology	Nuclear weapons Space weapons	Pollution	New technology is changing skill requirements at work
Economy	Recession Protectionism Resource shortages	Higher taxes Inflation Recession	Higher taxes Unemployment
Ecology	Warming Water shortages	Combat warming Continued reliance on coal and oil	Hurricanes Earthquakes Flooding
Politics	Hot war Trade war	Excessive regulation Inadequate regulation	Zoning Streets Development

Figure 9.3 - Examples of external threats.

It is a little hard to see how threats on the other side of the world might affect you, but if your country is involved in any way, even in simply defending against those threats, your personal taxes are probably affected. Conflicts around the world may restrict your employer's opportunities, may impact your travel choices, or may increase general tensions. It may be hard to see how you can do much about global warming, but if you see your community running low on water or dealing with severe weather changes, the impacts become clear.

That, briefly, is SWOT. It is a tool that will help you think about change as you think about the future. Just listing your strengths, weaknesses, opportunities, and threats is sufficient to get you thinking, but there is more. Look at your strengths to see how they match up with your opportunities. How can you use those strengths to enjoy the benefits of the opportunities that you have listed? What can you do to change what you perceive as your weaknesses? If you lack education in any area, can you get training, go back to school, or take courses online to change that weakness to strength? Those decisions will change your future.

THE FUTURES WHEEL

The futures wheel is a tool that is used by most futurists. It is also called a mind map and can be very simple, like the example below. Futures wheels can become complex as more levels are added. The futures wheel is very effective for brainstorming, whether you are working alone or in a group. You can draw one anywhere—on paper, on a whiteboard, or in your computer.

The idea is to start with a simple question or problem, then branch out from that idea to directly related ideas, effect, impacts, or whatever you are looking for.

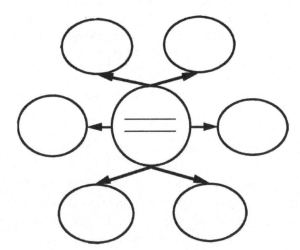

Figure 9.4 - A basic futures wheel showing spaces for the
first level of impacts.

.Here is an example of a personal futures wheel, starting with your original idea, expanding to your six domains.

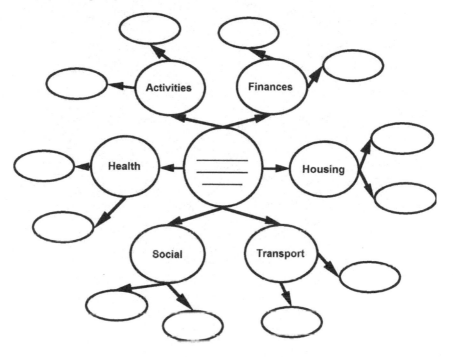

Figure 9.5 - A personal futures wheel with the six personal domains shown at the first level.

From each of the direct impacts in the first ring around your main question or idea, branch again to secondary ideas or impacts.

Figure 9.6 - A personal futures wheel expanded to the
second level of impacts.

Then branch again to a third ring of impacts. When you are drawing on
paper or on a whiteboard, futures wheels start getting messy at this level, but
they still work!

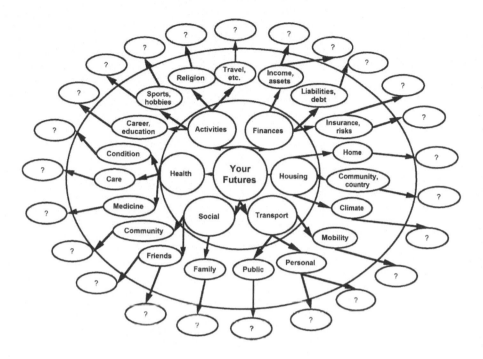

Figure 9.7 - A personal futures wheel
expanded to the third ring of impacts.

The futures wheel is very versatile. You will find it helpful in sorting out ideas or simply thinking about the future or other concepts. If you have occasion to speak to a group at school or at work, the futures wheel is a great tool for brainstorming and collecting ideas or information. All you need is a blank space and something to write with.

In this chapter you have learned how to use two more tools that will help you to understand more about yourself and your life. What you have learned will be very useful when you get to the chapters on developing scenarios and personal strategic planning.

Step Two

That was step one! Now you should know something more about your life and your future!

This research into your life will provide the foundation you need to explore and plan for your future. It is the same process that professional futurists go through when they work with organizations of all sizes to prepare for the future. They research the firm. Research the industry. Research the systems. Research the internal forces. Research the external forces. After all of the research is complete, the futurist can start working on the organization's futures—plural. Because there will be more than one plausible future. There are many plausible futures available, and that is what step two is about: exploring your futures using the scenario method.

Exploring plausible futures is the core method in preparing for the future. This exploration brings the important elements of the future together and in perspective. Having this knowledge about plausible futures gives you real targets and real, plausible situations that you can prepare for and plan for. But planning is step three.

So now on to step two: "Exploring Your Future with Scenarios"!

CHAPTER 10

Exploring Your Futures with Scenarios

Concept/Method

THE scenario method is based on the theory of alternative futures. Stated simply: If the future is *not* fully predetermined, then more than one future must be available. Based on that concept, you will explore and construct four different types of futures. The basic events may be the same, but the scenarios will be changed by the driving forces in your life.

Herman Kahn is credited with originating the scenario method during the 1950s, but the successful use of scenarios by Shell Oil on an international scale brought the scenario method to the attention of the business community and governments worldwide. Peter Schwartz's 1991 book, *The Art of the Long View,* detailed a system for developing scenarios based on the Shell approach. This book is still on most futurists' bookshelves.

Before we go into more detail about scenarios, this is a good place to make an important point. The Chinese philosopher Lao Tzu wrote in the sixth century BC:

Those who have knowledge don't predict.
Those who predict don't have knowledge.

The point is that scenarios will teach you quite a bit about what *may* happen in the future, but they do not tell you what *will* happen. Scenarios are not predictions. Most futurists will agree that they cannot predict the future, but they can make some pretty good guesses. That is what scenarios are meant to be: educated guesses about the future. What you have learned about your life in step one of this book is the foundation on which your personal scenarios will be based.

What Is a Scenario?

Let's start at the beginning to explain what a scenario is. First, scenario development is a method futurists use to explore plausible and wild card futures. Each scenario is a story about the future, say ten years from now. Scenarios are based on real knowledge, but it is the knowledge that is available now, in the present; you will create alternative scenarios to account for changes that may occur between the present and the time of the scenario, ten years away. In this section on scenarios, you will be working with four different types of scenarios about the future.

1. A continuation of the present into the future. This scenario assumes no major changes in the forces in your life during the next ten years.
2. Best plausible scenario. In this scenario, everything goes right for you. You will base this scenario on the extrapolations that you made for each of your personal domains. This scenario uses the optimistic projections for each of your domains.
3. Wild card or aspirational scenario. This scenario can be positive or negative and is drawn from events outside the cone of uncertainty for one of your domains. This can be a high-impact event or something important that you aspire to achieve.
4. A worst plausible scenario. In this scenario, everything goes wrong in your life. Here you will use the lower (negative) lines from your extrapolations.

As mentioned earlier, there are at least a dozen ways to create scenarios; some simple, some complex. We are going to use a simple approach that is very effective, yet easy to understand and use. These scenarios will become plausible stories about your future, stories that *could* happen, and you will be the main character in each. So this entire section, step two, is about exploring the future. Your future.

Professional futurists, when developing scenarios for a business or a governmental organization, may develop *many* different scenario outlines, testing several forces against each other until they come up with the combination that seems to give them the best array of plausible futures, dealing with the important forces and events. If you asked, you would probably find that most futurists use the two-axis matrix as an important tool in testing different forces against each other, identifying the "logics" for the final scenarios. This technique is detailed in *The Art of the Long View*, mentioned earlier. After testing a lot of scenarios, the professional futurist will write out detailed scenarios in story form.

You will follow a similar but simpler route. The professional futurist is usually working with an organization of thousands of people, while you will be making scenarios for yourself and your family. That gives you the advantage of simplicity and the power of decision making. You will focus on four scenarios here, but you can make as many as you want. After you have done the basic four scenarios, try creating scenarios using different external (STEEP) forces with each of your six domains, Be imaginative! Imagine the worst, then imagine the best. Imagine the surprises!

BOUNDING THE FUTURE

Since scenarios are about understanding what may happen in the future, we try to put boundaries on the future. We do this first with an optimistic scenario (the best plausible scenario) and then with a pessimistic scenario (the worst plausible scenario). Your real future should lie somewhere between those two.

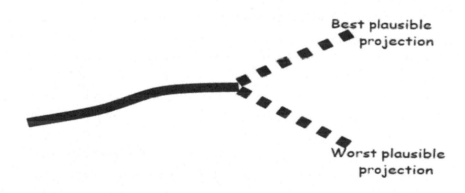

Figure 10.1 - The cone of uncertainty is the space between the best and worst plausible projections. That is where your plausible futures exist.

Be prepared: The future will probably not match any of your scenarios! No matter how careful you are in crafting your scenarios, the future will very likely be different. The value of the scenario is not precision; rather, the goal is to make pathways into the future so that you can recognize where you are when you get there. If, as the future unfolds, you see that reality is more positive than your extension of the present scenario, but not as positive as your optimistic scenario, you will recognize where you are and how reality compares with your scenarios.

WHAT CAUSES CHANGE IN SCENARIOS?

The challenge of scenario development is in looking from now into the future. The first question to ask is, "What can change?" Notice that question is asking "can," not "will." Nobody knows what *will* change, so keep asking, "What *can* change?" The next question is "Why?" In short, you want to know what can realistically change in the future, and what might cause that change to occur.

Primarily, change in your life will be created by forces, either internal forces (your six personal domains) or external forces (the STEEP categories). You have already looked closely at your personal domains and (if you are using the workbook) have projected where those domains might go in the future and which domains are likely to dominate the next ten years of your life.

The first scenario you develop might be one without any major change—just an extension of the present into the future. Certainly, there will be *some* change. You and your family will get older, start new life stages, and pass through the normal life events. In ten years, you will look a little different in the mirror, but life will all be familiar, no wrenching changes. But this scenario without much change will give you a standard, a way to compare the other scenarios.

In your other scenarios, there will be change, and that change will be driven by the forces in one or two of your personal domains. For example, the activities domain, which includes your work or career, is a dominant force during much of most people's lives. Specifically, your work or career tends to be the dominant driver from your thirties (or earlier) on to retirement. If your career is as a homemaker, it may start sooner and last much longer but become less dominant. So this is a good place to start asking yourself, "What could change?" What are the best things that could happen to your career over the next ten years? What are the worst things that could plausibly happen?

Outside forces may impose change on your life that will impact one or all of your domains. During 2008 and 2009, millions of people lost their jobs in a worldwide recession. Businesses collapsed, investments lost value, and many families lost their homes, their cars, and most of their possessions. Some had help from government programs such as unemployment compensation, but many people had no help at all. In the United States, large communities were formed by people living in tents because they had lost their homes. In China, workers in the cities returned to rural communities to stay with family and friends. Similar scenarios took place in much of the world.

Young people who were just starting their careers or were new to the workforce were often the first to lose their jobs. Students graduating from high schools, technical schools, and universities found themselves in a world that offered them very few good jobs or opportunities.

That is an example of change—big, externally driven change. That is one thing to look for in scenarios. What could change, and how would it impact your life?

Not all change is bad. As the world pulls out of a recession, new opportunities become apparent. New jobs, career opportunities, promotions, investments. This is also change but in a positive direction, which illustrates why you will make multiple scenarios. Try to anticipate the good things that can happen as well as the bad things that can impact your futures.

You must pay attention to the external forces, because they often directly impact your internal forces, your personal domains.

In the next chapter, you will learn how to set up your base of information for each of your scenarios; then in the following chapter, you will see how the changing forces in your world can shape your scenarios and your future.

CHAPTER 11

Building Your Base Scenario

CONCEPT

A base scenario assumes that during the time of the scenario, there are no big changes in the forces in your life, that the driving forces continue moving in their present directions. This scenario provides the foundation for other scenarios in which the forces may be very positive, very negative, or changed by a wild card event.

The first decision you have to make about your scenarios is when the scenario period will end. Are you exploring to the end-of-life stage or for the next ten years? What year will be the target year for your scenarios? The reason you need to decide on your target date now is that everything that will take place in your scenarios will happen between now and that target date.

With your target date for your scenarios in mind, this chapter will focus on life stages and the events that may occur in those stages. This will become the base information for you and your family members in each of your scenarios.

LIFE STAGES

If you are using the *Personal Futures Workbook* or the *Life Stages Worksheet* in Excel, you will already have the life stage information for your target year for yourself, your family members, and any other stakeholders who will be influential in your life over the next ten years. You will know the ages and life stages for each of the people who are likely to influence your life from now until your target date. Assuming you have picked a target date ten years in the future, you already know that every person who will impact or influence your life will be ten years older than they are today. What you should be looking for here are the implications for each person, including you, of being ten years older. What changes will that ten-year period bring to their lives and yours?

Stakeholders, Ages, and Stages

You. What life stage will you be in and what will be different for you at your target date because of a change in your age and life stage? Obviously you will be a little older, a little more experienced, and probably noticing some physical changes.

Your spouse. What age and life stage will your spouse be in at your target date, and what changes or impacts will result?

Your children. Children grow up fast, and ten years will make a big difference. Grade-schoolers may be off to college, and today's teen-agers may be starting families of their own in ten years. No matter their ages, children will continue to have impacts on your life, and their life stages will give you clues as to what those impacts may be. Their marriages, the arrival of your grandchildren, and the problems or joys in their lives will all have impacts on your life.

Your parents and your spouse's parents. What ages and life stages will your parents and your spouse's parents be in at your target year? What will be the big events in their lives in ten years? Retirement? Health problems? Will you and your spouse have to help them in some way? What events in your parents' lives will impact your life?

Close friends and family members. Ten years can affect relationships, but so can distance. Some of your close friends may be far away in ten years, or the interests that brought you together may change. Fortunately, email and other methods of communication are able to keep friendships together regardless of where those friends may be physically. At the same time, ten years provides plenty of time to develop new friendships and new interests.

People who are influential in your life. The term influential can have either a positive or a negative connotation. The mentor who has helped guide your career may be retired by your target date, but then the coworker or boss who inflicts some misery on you today may be long gone in ten years. The pastor in your church who has been such a friend may be transferred to a new church and helping others in a few years. How will the ages and stages of these influentials in your life be likely to change with time, and how will that impact your life?

Look back over those last few paragraphs again and try to think about the people in your life and the effects that time may have on each of them, as well as on you and your future.

EVENTS

This information from your life stages and life events will provide a foundation that will be the same in each of your scenarios. The differences between your scenarios will be determined by the driving forces in your life and in the world around you.

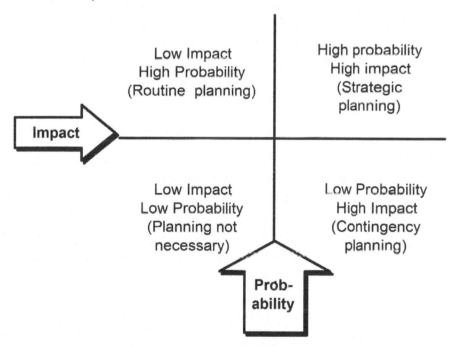

Figure 11.1 - Scenarios focus primarily on high-impact, high-probability events, although wild card scenarios are based on low-probability, high-impact events.

The Four Quadrants of the Impact/Probability Matrix:

Low-impact, low-probability events (lower-left quadrant). These are the
events that are unlikely to happen, but if they do, they will have
very little impact on your life, so there is really no reason to plan or
prepare for them.
Examples: For most people, parking tickets or traffic tickets are
minor events with little or no impact unless they become a habit.
They may be an annoyance, but they have little impact on your life.
Many events are similar—they are not likely to happen but will have
little or no impact if they do.

Low-impact, high-probability events (upper-left quadrant).
Examples: Birthdays, anniversaries, start of school, etc. These are
the events that you put on your calendar, but they generally do not
change your life because they are routine. Completing, filing, and
paying your taxes every year may be painful, but it is routine and
low impact—unless you forget to do it and get a visit from the tax
collectors!

High-probability, high-impact events (upper-right quadrant). The events
in this quadrant are the ones you will plan for and make strategies to
deal with. These are the events that will appear in your scenarios and
in your strategic plan.
Examples: Marriage, birth of a child, divorce, start of a new career,
retirement, and change of a life stage are all examples of high-impact
events that have a high probability of occurring.

High-impact, low-probability events (lower-right quadrant). Futurists call
events in this quadrant wild cards. They are not likely to happen,
but if they do, they will have a big impact on your life. These are the
events that will appear in your contingency plan.

Examples: Death of a family member, divorce, or being fired from your
job are all high-impact events, although for some people one or more of these
events may have a higher probability, moving it into the upper quadrant.

Natural events such as earthquakes, massive storms, or hurricanes may be events that occur only occasionally in the area where you live but are threats that are always possible. In parts of the world, terrorist acts or war are low-probability threats with devastating impacts. I live near the Gulf Coast of Texas, where hurricanes are a threat every year. I have had a contingency plan for a long time, so when Hurricane Dolly struck in the summer of 2008, we were prepared with a plan and a backup.

Not all wild card events are negative, but disasters are the events that people tend to think of first. Winning the lottery or other windfalls, multiple births (triplets or more), participating in a great adventure or outsize rewards or successes for something you have done are all examples of positive wild cards.

There is one other type of event that futurists have started considering as an alternative to writing wild card scenarios, and that is the "aspirational" event. Aspirational events are usually the result of setting a very high goal and then attempting to achieve it. Like the wild card, there is a low probability of success, but a big impact if successful. Lindberg's solo flight across the Atlantic would be an example of a successful aspirational event.

THE "EXTENDING THE PRESENT INTO THE FUTURE" SCENARIO

For your first scenario, the high-probability, high-impact events that may occur in your life and in the lives of your stakeholders over the next ten years will provide the main elements. You can call this scenario an "extension of the present" scenario because it will not be driven by any of the forces of major change.

Below is an example of a scenario worksheet from the *Personal Futures Workbook*. There will be several more examples of worksheets in this and other chapters, so in order to keep continuity, the worksheet examples will be based on the life of one person, Jan, a twenty-year-old university student.

Personal Domains	"Extending the Present into the Future" scenario—Potential high-impact, high-probability events
Activities	Complete education, training Start work, career Career advancement, promotion
Finances	First long-term income Fully responsible for debts, bill, investments, savings, taxes Mortgage Insurance
Health	Mental and physical maturity
Housing	First home and related responsibilities
Social	Leave parent's home Marry First child and parental responsibilities
Transportation	Fully responsible for personal and family transportation

Figure 11.2 - An example of a scenario worksheet completed by a twenty-year-old university student.

This example tells you quite a bit about the next ten years for Jan, a twenty-year-old university student. Jan will continue to be our example through the rest of these worksheets. To the table of events above, add that Jan values honesty, commitment, and family. Jan also has goals that include two children (eventually) and an executive-level position by age thirty. If you happen to be twenty, this could be your life! But, regardless of your age, you can almost see this person's life unfolding toward age thirty.

Now pretend that this person has reached age thirty, ten years from now, and is sitting down to write a story about life over the past ten years. You can probably see that with the information in the table and the details from one's imagination, writing a short story about this person's future should not be difficult.

That is how you start your personal scenarios. Fill in the scenario worksheet, then write a story about your future. Your first scenario (extending the present into the future) becomes the basis for all of other scenarios. For each of your other scenarios, simply change this base scenario by adding one or two forces of change. One scenario will be driven by positive change, the next will be driven by negative change, and the last will be driven by low-probability, high-impact change. The next chapter goes into detail, showing how driving forces change your futures.

CHAPTER 12

Driving Forces Will Change the Directions of Your Scenarios

CONCEPT

YOUR scenarios are steered by the driving forces in your life and in the world around you. The two-axis matrix is an effective tool for analyzing driving forces and showing how they relate to each other.

In this chapter, you are going to manipulate your future. Actually, what you manipulate will be your *views* of your future, but you will see how changes in the forces in your life can change your future. Understanding how one set of forces in your life can impact other forces to bring about change in your life will probably give you a sense of some power over your future. That is good, because that should inspire you to learn to use these tools well.

For the rest of your scenarios, you will continue with the same worksheet information that you developed for your "continuation of the present" scenario, because this base information will be the same in all of your scenarios. The differences between your scenarios will be in the driving forces in your life, both the internal forces and the external forces. Think about that for a second. Once you have figured out what the high-impact, high-probability events are for the next ten years of your life, they will be high probability no matter what else is happening. Whether your career is skyrocketing or falling in the pits, the high-probability events are still events that you must be prepared to deal with.

Some expected events may not happen. For example, marriage and a first child are very common events during one's twenties. However, forces in your life or in the world might cause marriage or children to be postponed. If either or both of those events are postponed, that will affect the next stage of your life. Either event could occur in the adult stage, or either might not occur at all. Other events may also be altered by the changing forces in your life.

In this chapter, you will explore your personal domains, the *internal* forces in your life, as well as the *external*, or STEEP forces. For our examples, we will continue to use the worksheets completed by Jan, a twenty-year-old student who aspires to a career in writing or publishing.

The Positive Scenario

First, you will develop your positive scenario. The worksheet in figure 12.1 has all of the same information as the worksheet for your extending the present scenario, so you will simply convert that to a positive scenario by adding information about the forces in your personal domains.

Think back to the extrapolations we discussed in chapter 3 for each of your personal domains. For each domain, you made a positive (best plausible) extrapolation and a negative (worst plausible) extrapolation. Below, in figure 12.2 are positive extrapolations for twenty-year-old Jan written out in worksheet form. These examples may seem a little vague, but we are exploring a ten-year period, so you will be working within the entire range of positive yet plausible futures.

Personal Domains	Potential high-impact, high-probability events (from base scenario)	Positive scenario— Assumptions from extrapolations
Activities	Complete education, training Start work, career Career advancement, promotion	Extremely good job
Finances	First long-term income Fully responsible for debts, bill, investments, savings, taxes Mortgage Insurance	Very high pay and benefits
Health	Mental and physical maturity	Continued very good health

Housing	First home and related responsibilities	Very nice home in very good area (or country)
Social	Leave parents' home Marry First child and parental responsibilities	Very good family life—no problems with family or stakeholders
Transport or mobility	Fully responsible for personal and family transportation	Really nice car and short commute

Figure 12.1 - Jan's worksheet showing assumptions for a positive scenario.

When you add assumptions about your personal domains to the major events that you expect to occur over the next ten years, it is easy to see how the positive assumptions change the nature of the scenario.

Now look at the outside forces that may impact your life over the next ten years, using the same format as you have with personal domains in figure 12.2. Choose the most optimistic outlooks for each category of forces.

External forces	Positive scenario, STEEP assumptions
Social	Substantial advancements in reducing poverty, caring for poor
Technological	Huge advances in medicine, biology, and medical tech Substantial advances in energy, robotics, nanotech
Ecological	Global warming—the climate remains stable without additional warming
Economic	Rising worldwide economy
Political	No new wars, existing conflicts winding down

Figure 12.2 - STEEP categories with optimistic projections.

Of these projections, the rising world economy over the next ten years will probably have a direct impact on Jan's future, directly affecting both job opportunities and finances. You can reasonably compare Jan's projections with your own life, as these projections may relate to your own future.

Technology advances will probably have direct impacts for both you and your stakeholders—all of them; family, friends, coworkers, and organizations. The impacts of the other categories will probably be more indirect, based on these projections.

You can probably already see how this positive scenario will shape up. It will be optimistic but within plausible limits. As you lay out your own scenarios, keep asking yourself questions about what the next ten years could bring, but keep the answers within plausibility. Dream, imagine, be creative, but stay within the limits of what could reasonably be expected to happen in your life over the next ten years.

With that in mind, look at a two-axis matrix that diagrams two key forces in life, careers (in the activities domain), and family life (in the social domain).

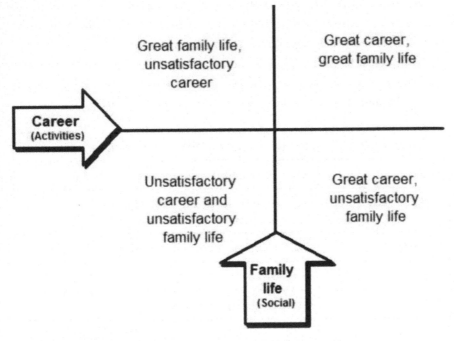

Figure 12.3 - A two-axis matrix showing plausible plots for your scenarios.

The matrix diagram shows a different story in each quadrant. Very brief stories, but each can be the starting point for a plausible scenario. In this diagram, the best outcome is found in the upper-right quadrant, and that is your story for your positive scenario, "Great career, great family life."

The Negative Scenario

For the negative scenario, use the same basic information as the first two scenarios, but now the projections for the personal domains will all be based on the "worst plausible" projections. Here are some projections for Jan, our twenty-year-old example.

Personal Domains	Potential high-impact, high-probability events (from base scenario)	Negative scenario— Assumptions from extrapolations
Activities	Complete education, training Start work, career Career advancement, promotion	Unable to get a job for which I'm trained and educated
Finances	First long-term income Fully responsible for debts, bill, investments, savings, taxes Mortgage Insurance	Still working at entry level or minimum wage work
Health	Mental and physical maturity	Health still good except for high frustration
Housing	First home and related responsibilities	Still living with parents at 30
Social	Leave parents' home Marry First child and parental responsibilities	Marriage and family on hold until affordable
Transport or mobility	Fully responsible for personal and family transportation	Same car I drove in high school. Commuting by bus or train

Figure 12.4 - Worksheet showing negative assumptions for a scenario.

This takes Jan in a very different direction, to the lowest limits of plausibility as seen today. But this *is* plausible, and should be considered as a reasonable scenario, because the events are similar to those faced by millions of people in 2009.

External forces	Negative or pessimistic STEEP assumptions
Social	Discontent seems everywhere No one seems to have quite enough
Technological	Change is very slow Many promising technologies just don't seem to get to the market place
Ecological	Warming is increasing faster than expected Needed technologies are not yet economic
Economic	Economy is still very slow Not enough jobs and too many over-qualified applicants
Political	Promises, argument, and blame, but no positive change Political brinksmanship risks war

Figure 12.5 - STEEP categories with Jan's pessimistic projections.

If you look back at the matrix diagram in figure 12.4, you will see a title for Jan's negative scenario in the lower-left quadrant, "Unsatisfactory career and unsatisfactory family life."

Now add in negative assumptions for the world and the surrounding community, and twenty-year-old Jan is looking at a very challenging future if this scenario should actually occur. This helps to illustrate why you will create four different scenarios. In the first three scenarios, you are putting boundaries around the future. You will have one scenario that extends the present into the future without major change, a second scenario that describes your best plausible future (top boundary), and a third scenario that describes the worst plausible future (bottom boundary). Your fourth scenario (wild card) will be outside the boundaries.

THE WILD CARD SCENARIO

For the wild card scenario, forget about plausibility. Now you are talking about whatever may be possible in your life over the next ten years. You can make many versions of the wild card scenario, and it is a good idea to make more than one or two. Again, twenty-year-old Jan's thoughts about the future will provide your examples.

Personal Domains	Potential high-impact, high-probability events (from base scenario)	Wild card scenario possibilities
Activities	Complete education, training Start work, career Career advancement, promotion	My hobby becomes my profession—successfully
Finances	First long-term income Fully responsible for debts, bill, investments, savings, taxes Mortgage Insurance	Extreme wealth Extreme poverty
Health	Mental and physical maturity	Disabled by severe illness or injury
Housing	First home and related responsibilities	Relocate to another continent
Social	Leave parents' home Marry First child and parental responsibilities	Death of spouse before 30 Birth of quintuplets
Transport or mobility	Fully responsible for personal and family transportation	Totally reliant on public transportation—positive or negative

Figure 12.6 - Table showing possible wild card events in personal domains for a twenty-year-old.

Jan's wild card worksheet shows high-impact, low-probability events within each personal domain that might occur before age thirty, Jan's target year. Each is possible, each would have a strong impact, and none is very *likely* to occur. They provide a space for thinking about the futures that you do not expect—but *could* happen.

Now that you are looking beyond plausible futures, what are your *possible* futures? Will Earth be struck by an asteroid? Will global warming turn to cooling and a new ice age? Will people live healthy lives of 150 to 200 years, or more? Will you be able to live forever inside a computer? All of these possible futures have been seriously suggested by knowledgeable people. In fact, the possible futures are, like stars, beyond count.

Some people take the ostrich approach to wild cards. They simply ignore them because they cannot deal with a future with no limits. So how do you put boundaries on the possible futures? Start with the possible futures that affect you. Weigh the probabilities. Our definition of wild cards includes the phrase, "low probability." How low?

I mentioned earlier that one of my personal wild cards is hurricanes. I believe that a hurricane may find me here in South Texas once in twenty to twenty-five years, a 4–5 percent risk. That is low probability, but it is a much higher probability than an asteroid strike. Futurists consider the odds, but they are also alert to signals of change in the world.

In the next table, Jan considers possible, high-impact events that could occur in the world or in the community over the next ten years.

External forces	Wild card scenario. Positive and negative STEEP possibilities
Social	Revolution against extremism Lifespan exceeds 120
Technological	Cures or preventions for most major diseases Solar becomes major source of energy Auto industry abandons internal combustion engines Worldwide Internet crash
Ecological	Global warming accelerates World responds to warming threat with drastic change and tech Natural disaster (hurricane, fire, tornado, earthquake, flood, etc.) strikes here at home
Economic	Global currency Extreme inflation Food shortages
Political	World peace Nuclear war

Figure 12.7 - STEEP categories with wild card possibilities.

Sometimes it is tempting to select one event and build a scenario around it, which is okay, but events and forces tend to affect each other. One force may accelerate another force, as wind accelerates fire, while a different force, rain, would dampen and slow the fire. Any of the events shown in these two tables could provide the change forces for a complete scenario, but by placing two events into a two-axis matrix, you can set up some interesting wild card scenarios, as you will see a little later in this chapter. Futurists commonly test several forces against each other to see how the forces interact.

The Aspirational Scenario

The aspirational scenario is unique. Like the other scenarios, it is set on the same background of anticipated high-impact events, but this scenario is about choice and determination. Notice that Jan has only made two entries for the aspirational scenario. Two are enough.

Personal Domains	Potential high-impact, high-probability events (from base scenario)	Aspirations—high- impact, low probability
Activities	Complete education, training Start work, career Career advancement, promotion	Write a best seller (book, movie, song, game, program, etc.)
Finances	First long-term income Fully responsible for debts, bill, investments, savings, taxes Mortgage Insurance	Achieve financial independence before 30
Health	Mental and physical maturity	
Housing	First home and related responsibilities	
Social	Leave parents' home Marry First child and parental responsibilities	
Transportation	Fully responsible for personal and family transportation	

Figure 12.8 - Worksheet showing
one individual's aspirations for the future.

"Write a best seller" sets a huge goal for a twenty year old, and that outsize goal could become a force in this person's life. The additional goal of achieving financial independence by age thirty is also huge. Both goals are low probability, but others have achieved the same goals in their twenties (author Ken Kesey, for example). Both goals have high impacts and would transform Jan's life.

Take a look at these goals from a different direction using the futurists' traditional tool, the two-axis matrix.

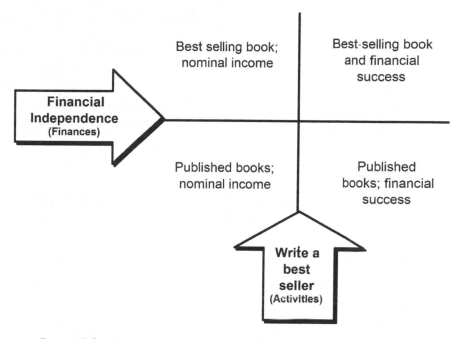

Figure 12.9 - A matrix showing how Jan's two aspirations might interact.

You can see that there is a story about Jan's future in each of the four quadrants. There is an assumption that Jan will write books but that the levels of success may vary. The upper-right quadrant holds Jan's preferred future, and that is the story that will become Jan's aspirational scenario.

You now have examples of five different types of scenarios that you can use as models to guide you as you develop your own scenarios.

- Continuation of the present scenario
- Positive or best plausible scenario
- Negative or worst plausible scenario
- Wild card scenario
- Aspirational scenario

With these models as a starting point, use the two-axis matrix to match any two forces you can imagine. As you practice this process, you will recognize that the matrix is a very powerful tool.

Examples Using the Two-axis Matrix

Here is a little more information about the two-axis matrix with two more examples. The first example will look a little farther ahead in your future to explore retirement.

This diagram represents two forces that are very common in most people's futures: retirement and family life. This diagram illustrates levels of satisfaction in these two areas.

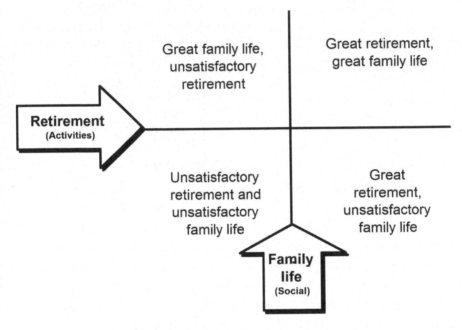

Figure 12.10 - This matrix shows four quadrants that result when the forces of retirement meet family life.

Above you see four descriptions of life based on these two domains. Here you have retirement representing the activities domain, because from the midsixties onward, the potential for retirement has existed in many people's lives. The other axis is family life, which is a driving force in the social domain. In the upper-left quadrant, family life is very good, but the retirement is unsatisfactory. Note that the quadrants do not explain why about anything. This is because the person creating the quadrant (you, for example) builds the definitions into the design, so you get to define for yourself what an unsatisfactory career or a great family life really means.

How could retirement be unsatisfactory? My research suggested many possibilities, but I first want to point out that most of the people in my research were very happy with this stage of their life, convinced that this was the best stage of all. On the other hand, some people were surprised to realize, when they stopped working, that they had also left their role in life, their career identity, behind. They had also left their workplace friends and a sizable piece of their social life. Many had to build new roles and new social networks.

Some new retirees had planned to play lots of golf but had no plans for anything else, so they had to develop new interests. A number of people, usually wives, were now caregivers for disabled spouses, and some retirees just had not saved enough money to live comfortably. Many of these people simply had not thought seriously about retirement and did not realize how much their life would change.

An important point here is that there is a real value in planning for your *whole* retirement, not just your financial retirement. Think about what you want to *do* in retirement that will keep you busy and give your life some purpose. You might even consider a second career, particularly if you see indications that you might live a very long life.

In the next matrix, career is on one axis and finances is on the other axis. That gives you a slightly different look at the forces at work in your life.

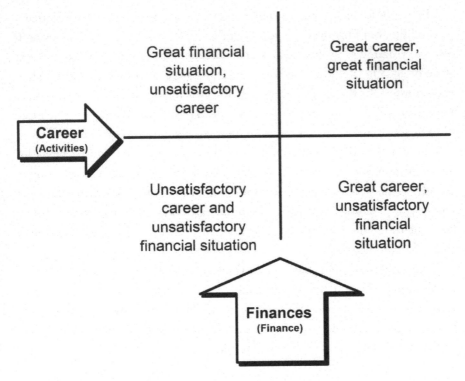

Figure 12.11 - This matrix shows four quadrants that result when the forces of one's career meet the forces (or realities) of one's financial situation.

This career/finances matrix illustrates four possible situations that could occur in your life at nearly any age. In the lower-right quadrant, you see that it is possible to have a good career, even a good income, and still not have a good financial situation. How could this be? That is a question that you should be asking yourself as you study any matrix, but here are some possibilities:

- Great financial situation, unsatisfactory career. This might be labeled "Great money, lousy job." The work could be dangerous or extremely stressful, or it might include very unpleasant coworkers. But you stay for the money!
- Great career, unsatisfactory financial situation. The financial situation could mean low pay, but it could also indicate that you have spent more than you can earn.

• The lower-left quadrant includes all of the above!

These are just a few quick examples, and you can probably think of lots more. The important thing is to ask which examples will fit your future. Keep asking yourself questions as you work with the matrix. Understanding these forces and doing some realistic planning for the future can help you avoid such difficulties.

The examples here should give you a pretty good feel for how the two-axis matrix works and how you can use it as a tool.

One caution about the two-axis-matrix. It is a great tool for developing and illustrating concepts, but it should not be construed as a mathematical or precise tool. Accept it for what it does very well, but do not try to fine tune your life or the matrix. Thinking about the future is meant to help you plan your quality of life, not pin life down to a schedule.

In the next chapter, you will create scenarios from all of the information that you have collected, turning them into short stories about your future.

CHAPTER 13

Telling Stories about Your Future

Concept

YOUR scenario structures are turned into stories about the future. The act of writing these scenarios reveals how forces and events interact and how each scenario develops over time.

This chapter is where you will actually create scenarios, stories about your life and your future. You have already gone through all the steps of thinking about what your future could be; now it is time to turn that information into stories about your future.

In my workshops, someone usually wonders why we should write out scenarios. "Don't we already have all the information for each scenario? Why do we need to write a story?"

My answer is that the information you have in your worksheet is just a list of possibilities. A scenario puts that information into a sequence, a series of causes and effects, a story about how life works. Then, everything fits together, a little like a completed puzzle.

By the end of the workshop, everyone has written four scenarios, and most are pretty proud of what they have accomplished. That helps to make the scenarios memorable, which is important. Over the coming years, remembering the different scenarios you have worked out will help you to see what is actually happening in your life, and that will prepare you to anticipate and adjust to whatever is coming next.

So, where do you start?

Everybody takes a little different approach, something that fits their way of thinking and organizing. Some people start with a title for the scenario, some start with a first sentence that leads the way into the scenario. Others make an outline, and some stare at the empty page for awhile, and then they start writing, letting their thoughts flow onto the page. Use whatever approach works for you, and I will try to help.

BEGINNINGS

The quadrants in a matrix should suggest some good plots. Look at your information from one scenario and see what it suggests. Jan, our twenty-year-old example, might start scenarios using one or more of these sentences:

- When I was twenty, I knew that I wanted to be writer, but I never imagined that the next ten years would unfold as they did.
- The past ten years have been the (worst, best, most interesting, etc.) of my life.
- The end of a decade is a good time to reflect on one's life, and when I reached thirty, I had a lot to reflect on.
- Ten years ago, I set some really big goals for my life, and as a result of those goals, the past ten years have been absolutely amazing.
- I think I can deal with nearly anything now, and the last ten years have taught me how.
- Sometimes I ask myself, "How did I get to this point in my life?"
- My thirtieth birthday was quite an event. I told my friends that I could finally see light at the end of the tunnel, and they laughed. "Look out, it's another train!"

Those should be enough opening lines to help you get started. From there, tell your story about what happened in your life over the past ten years as though you were just remembering it. Work in your information about the events and forces that you have considered for that particular scenario just as you might have experienced them, then add some imagination. You can make your scenarios short or long, but try to write them as though they are your story, your life. They may be!

Structure

A little structure may help you keep the story moving. Writers often say that a story must have a beginning, a middle, and an end. That approach can give you the framework for an outline:

> Opening: When I was twenty, I knew I wanted to be writer, but I never
>   imagined that the next ten years would unfold as they did.
> Beginning: What did you expect?
>   How did it start?
> Middle: What happened over the decade?
>   What forces caused the changes in your life?
>   What events occurred along the way?
> End: Where are you at the end of ten years?
>   What do you see in your future (the next ten years)?

Journalists traditionally try to answer six questions when they write a story: Who? What? When? Where? How? and Why?

The "Who?" is you, although some of your stakeholders may also be a part of your story. Most of these questions will be answered naturally, but it helps to be aware of them.

Finally, do not worry about your ability to write a story. You may be the only reader, and you are definitely the most important audience. These scenarios will be like maps for you in the future, because they show you the best, the expected, and the worst futures you might expect, plus one future you may not expect. As maps, they will show you different views of where you are and where you could be. You can constantly compare reality to your scenarios, and they will show you which forces are moving you in expected, or unexpected, directions.

Even if the forces that are changing your life are not the forces you wrote about in your scenarios, you will understand what has changed and what new forces are at work. Then you can analyze your situation and write new scenarios that reflect your new futures.

What else can scenarios do for you? Or what else can you do with scenarios?

LONG-TERM PERSPECTIVE.

As you start looking ten years ahead in your own life, you will start recognizing forces and patterns in the world around you—in your work or profession, in your community, and in your country. Seeing the forces of change as they move through your world can help you to anticipate the good changes and the troublesome changes. This anticipation, or foresight, reduces the number of surprise situations that may put you on the defensive, forcing you to react. Whenever you can deal with events before they happen, before they become a problem, you have some control and usually time to think and prepare for whatever the situation may be.

Recognize what is important. There are many events in our lives and careers that are simply not important. Recognizing what is really important in your life will help you sleep better because you will not be worrying about things that do not really make a difference in your life. Sometimes, our reactions to unimportant events make a greater difference than the events themselves. You may find it helpful when faced with a stressful situation to ask yourself if this is really important. Will it make a difference a year from now?

Use mini-scenarios to make decisions. When you face a decision, ask yourself, "What's the worst thing that can happen? What's the best thing that can happen? What could happen that would be a real surprise?" Ask again. Is that really the best? Really the worst? Now you have a little more information to help you make your decision.

Use the two-axis matrix. You can draw this on a napkin or an envelope. Anywhere. While a graduate student, I once attended a meeting of professional futurists in which eight of us sat at a round table listening to the speaker. At some point, I realized that each person at the table had drawn a matrix, showing the forces the speaker was describing. The matrix is a tool that can be used at any level. Just pick two forces and see where they could go in relation to each other. Practice with this tool and you will be surprised by the insights that you will develop.

Be aware of existing scenarios. If your organization or your community develops scenarios, often used in strategic planning, find out about them. Read the scenarios and understand them. Do you agree with them as plausible futures? Are they up to date? Do you see different scenarios? These scenarios may represent the thinking of management in your organization or your community, and that thinking may impact your life. Awareness can be an important ally in dealing with the future.

That pretty well sums up this section on exploring change and exploring the future with scenarios. Now you are ready to look at how to create your future or change your future with personal strategic planning.

Step Three

In step one, you learned about conducting research into your own life. These same principles apply anywhere, whether in your life, in a small business, or in a global organization. You must understand the stakeholders, the system, the events, and the forces, both internal and external, before you can start to understand the future.

In step two, you learned how to organize the information about your life to develop background events for your scenarios; then you applied internal and external forces to those same events to make very different scenarios that would help you understand some of the futures that might occur.

Now you are beginning step three, in which you will describe the future that you *want* to live. You will develop strategies to achieve that future while dealing with the high-impact, high-probability events that may occur along the way. Finally, you will develop strategies and contingency plans to deal with unexpected, high-impact events that may occur. Does that sound like a lot to undertake and achieve? Do not be at all intimidated. This will be just like the steps you have already gone through, in which you have achieved big things, one step at a time.

I was pretty young when I learned that lesson. As a matter of fact, it was my fifteenth birthday when I joined a group of friends to climb Mt. Hood, an 11,240-foot inactive volcano in Oregon. We started climbing from Timberline Lodge, at about 6000 feet. Hours later, and still a long way from the top, we were tired. Our leaders told us to just keep putting one foot in front of the other, and we would get there. Eventually we were kicking our crampons into the steep, icy chute just below the summit. We could see that we were near the top, and our energy returned. We reached the summit with enthusiasm and a little relief.

Obviously, I still remember that lesson—so I just keep putting one foot in front of the other. You already know that one step after another can accomplish big things, but you may be surprised at what you can accomplish in this next section.

CHAPTER 14

Personal Strategic Planning

CONCEPT

THE strategic planning process is simple: Develop a vision of the future that you want to achieve over time; develop strategies to achieve that vision; create a step-by-step, year-by-year plan for executing your strategies; draw up a contingency plan to deal with low-probability, high-impact events; and then follow the plan.

Whenever I conduct a workshop or speak to a group of people, I usually ask two questions. Both are about strategic planning.

The first question is, "Have you had any exposure to or experience with strategic planning, whether in your work, your community or somewhere else?" Usually about two-thirds of the group will raise their hands. They have had *some* experience with strategic planning.

The second question is directly to the point. "How many of you found that to be a positive experience?" Usually about one-third of the group raises their hands. About half of the people who have had experience with strategic planning found the experience to be positive. The figures are not precise, because it is what I can see from a stage, usually with lights in my eyes. However, it is a reasonable estimate, and it seems to be pretty consistent whether the group is a dozen or a thousand.

STRATEGIC PLANNING WORKS!

After these questions and answers, I emphasize to the group, "Strategic planning works!" I sincerely believe that, so I go on to explain why many people in the audience have not had a good experience with strategic planning, particularly at a large organization.

First, any large organization has multiple divisions, each with its own interests and agenda. The organization will also have individuals at all levels that have a personal interest in how a strategic plan might affect them. That means that there will be negotiations and jostling for advantage throughout the planning process. In order to arrive at agreements, there are usually many compromises. Second, for the same reasons, there may be bruising disputes. Third, some strategic plans are just plans. The planners have neglected to develop strategies. Finally, some strategic plans are not really implemented. There are other reasons as well, but you get the idea. Size can sometimes be a disadvantage.

So in strategic planning, small may be good, as there are fewer decision makers, fewer influences, and fewer disputes. In your personal life, the decision makers will usually be limited to one or two. That one factor makes a huge difference from planning in organizations. As a result, personal strategic planning can be *very* effective. Even if your plan goes into a drawer and seldom comes out, once you have gone through the process, the plan is stored in your memory.

THE PERSONAL STRATEGIC PLAN

So, what is a strategic plan, and how will you make one? A strategic plan is a long-term plan for your personal future that builds on the research you have done and the scenarios you have written in the previous sections. You will start your strategic plan by deciding what you want your future to be in ten years; then you will make strategies and plans to achieve that future, taking steps each year to make your plan and your vision a reality by the tenth year. To be more specific:

- First, you will think about and write down what you want your future to be in ten years. This is your vision of the future.
- Second, you will create strategies. They will be strategies to achieve

your vision of the future and strategies to deal with the high-probability or high-impact events that may occur over the next ten years.

- Third, you will create an action plan. This will be a schedule of actions that you will take each year to implement your strategies, moving you toward your vision of your future.
- Fourth, you will create a contingency plan. This will be a plan to deal with the low-probability, high-impact events that might threaten to disrupt your life.

That is your strategic plan in just four parts.

Even as you are creating your vision of your future, keep in mind that if you change your mind about what you want your future to be, you can change your vision and your plan. This is very important to remember, because your plan is like a pair of shoes. If your shoes become uncomfortable, change to a pair that fits and feels comfortable. If your vision and plan no longer fit what you want from the future, change the vision and the plan.

HOW STRATEGIC PLANNING WORKS

When you create your vision, you are defining what you *want* your future to be. You are also identifying a destination—the place where you want to be in your life ten years from now. That is the life you want to be living.

Once you spell out to yourself where you are going with your life, you can start making decisions about how to get there—how to reach your destination, your vision of the future. Strategies determine how you will get to the future and how you will deal with life events along the way. That is why this is called strategic planning.

It is all as simple as thinking about what you *want* to do and what you *have* to do over the next ten years, then developing strategies that will take you there. In this way, you will achieve what you want and accomplish whatever you must. This is simply a matter of figuring things out in advance so that you know what to do to get from now to ten years from now!

Once you have decided on your strategies to achieve your future, you can lay out a timeline for each strategy. The timeline will tell you when you are going to take each step toward executing your strategy over the next ten years. Some strategies may take the whole ten years while other strategies may take only a few years. Your action plan is like a ten-year calendar with all of your timelines spelled out so that you know when to take each step toward achieving your future.

If you accomplish each of the steps in each of your strategies within ten years, you should arrive at the future for which you planned. That is how strategic planning works—and it does work.

Now, what do you expect from the future? What is the future you *want* to be living ten years from now? In the next chapter you will be exploring that question in order to build your vision, your destination in the future.

CHAPTER 15

A Vision of Your Future

CONCEPT

To create a vision of your future, break your future into six parts: your six personal domains. Envision your future in each domain, then bring those six visions together into a vision of your life in the future.

In the academic worlds of futures studies and strategic planning and thinking, the term "vision" is a part of everyday conversation. When I started leading workshops about personal futures, I spoke briefly about personal "visions of the future." Then I asked the participants to write out a sentence or two about their vision of their own future, the future they wanted.

Whoa! They brought me to a full stop. "What *is* a vision? How do you figure this out? This isn't that simple!" I backed up and started over, and that is where we will start here.

WHAT IS A VISION?

What is a vision? In this book, we are talking about a vision or image of *your* future. What image do you have of your life at any time in the future? Ten, twenty, fifty years from now? That is one reason we started our exploration of your future with life stages, because seeing or observing other people's lives in each of life's stages helps you to build your own images of what life is typically like in those stages. When you visualize yourself in those stages, you will start thinking about what you like or do not like and what you want your own life to be in that stage. That is the *start* of building an image.

People in those early workshops understood that, but they wanted more detail. Specifically, they did not know what they really wanted in their lives ten years from now. To each of them this seemed like too big of a thing to handle with just a sentence or two. This was important! They needed a way to figure out what their vision should be, and I agreed.

I suggested that they break the vision project down into simple parts, starting with their personal domains. Look at each domain and ask, "What do I want my life to be in *this* domain?" With answers to that question in each of the domains, it was much easier for everyone to build a realistic image, or vision, of what they wanted for their future.

There was one more question about creating a vision that came up in different workshops. "Why? Why do I need a vision of my future?"

A Vision Is a Destination

That question is a little easier to answer. The future, your future, is a destination, a place in time. You have to choose a destination for your future, because if you do not, you will not have much say in what your future will be.

It is a little like planning a vacation. When you decide to take a vacation, one of the earliest decisions is "Where?" Where will you go? Until you make that decision, you cannot do much to make plans, reservations, or other arrangements. If you decide to travel to Paris for your vacation, you can then think about the places you will visit in Paris as well as where you might stop on the way to or from Paris or while in the city. These are also destinations, part of your trip. This planning is very much like imagining your future and the things you want to do there.

But what if you change your mind? What if you decide that you want to go to Bangkok instead?

Just as you can change your vacation destination, you can change your vision for your future. If you see that the prospects for your organization are fading, you can change. If you work in an industry that is overloaded with talent but has declining opportunities, you can change. If your vision was to retire at age sixty, but you think you would be either bored or short of money, change your vision. It is very important that you remember that this is *your* vision, *your* plan, and *your* future. You can change anything at any time, so you should be prepared to change whether because of a change in your interests or changes in the world around you.

Now, back to building your vision of the future. Below is an example of a worksheet from the *Personal Futures Workbook*, filled in for Jan, our twenty-year-old example who is building a vision for life at age thirty.

	Your ten-year vision for each domain
Activities- What do you want to do in your career, retirement, religion, travel, sports, hobbies, etc.?	Writing and publishing. Books, short stories, fiction and nonfiction. Traveling to do research for my writing.
Finances- What's important financially; income, net worth, investments, insurance, etc.?	Financially comfortable, living an upper middle-class life, investing for retirement.
Health- How will you protect your health? What medical care will you need?	Exercising every day, stretching, weights, fast walking. Protecting my joints, eyes, etc. Healthy diet, watching my weight, regular physicals
Housing- Where will you be living?	San Francisco area, probably North Bay, small, single-family home.
Social- Who will be close or important to you?	Married and expecting our first child. Close to our parents, who won't be retired yet.
Transportation- What transportation will you need?	Bicycles locally, husband commuting by ferry, hopefully an electric car for longer trips.

Figure 15.1 - Jan's worksheet for developing a vision.

There is nothing dramatic in this vision of Jan's future, but clearly, Jan anticipates a successful and comfortable lifestyle.

One other question came up in the workshops. I was asked if our vision should be the same as our optimistic scenario. The answer is that your vision is about what you *want* your future to be, not necessarily about what your scenarios showed your life *could* be.

After you decide on your vision for ten years in the future, take another look at that vision worksheet. This time, instead of looking ten years ahead, think about your life in later years, say in your seventies or eighties. This will give you a little different perspective (unless you are already near seventy) than your ten-year vision. Below is another example for Jan at age twenty; looking ahead to age seventy five, which happens to be Jan's grandfather's age. The grandfather provides a model or an image of the independent life stage at age seventy-five.

	Your vision for each domain for age seventy-five
Activities- What do you want to do in your career, retirement, religion, travel, sports, hobbies, etc.?	Still writing and traveling to conduct research for more writing. The pace and pressure to produce has slowed, and much more discretionary time is available.
Finances- What's important financially; income, net worth, investments, insurance, etc.?	Mortgage is paid, spending requirements have declined, and investments have weathered the economic ups and downs quite well. Wills have been written to provide orderly transition of our estate. Financial plan for 100 and beyond.
Health- How will you protect your health? What medical care will you need?	Still very healthy, though having more checkups and tests and taking some regular medications. Still careful of diet and weight and still exercising regularly. On track to live beyond one hundred. Have written DNRs and instructions to physicians.
Housing- Where will you be living?	Still living in North Bay although we've explored possibilities around the world. We both plan to remain at home in the event of terminal illness, if possible, but have identified an elder living facility if necessary.
Social- Who will be close or important to you?	Grandparents have died, but all four parents are still living and healthy, approaching age one hundred. Two children and four grandchildren live near Santa Barbara, close enough to see frequently. Great grandchildren expected soon! We have strong supportive social networks here at home.
Transportation- What transportation will you need?	Still riding bikes locally. If I get wobbly, I'll get a three-wheeler! Our second electric car is over twenty-five years old. Good public transport from our neighborhood available if we have to stop driving, but not likely soon.

Figure 15.2 - Jan's vision for life at age seventy-five.

Again, no dramatic changes, but a vision that gives Jan guidance and goals in many areas. Most importantly, the worksheet gives Jan a clear image of a future that is fifty years away. This vision also gives Jan plenty of time to adjust the image to meet the impacts of change, particularly in the medical and technological fields.

The final step in creating your visions of the future is to condense the visions for each of the six personal domains into two statements—one for your ten-year vision, and one for your independent stage vision.

Following are Jan's examples of envisioning the future at age twenty.

My vision of life at age thirty finds me married and expecting our first child soon; healthy, active, and enjoying a productive writing career; working from our home in the North Bay; and pursuing a green life.

My vision of life at age seventy-five finds me still married and in the same home, writing and traveling, still healthy, enjoying our parents in their older years as well as our children and grandchildren. Life is more relaxed but pleasantly active, and we still pursue a long, healthy green life.

Both statements are simple and easy to remember but clearly represent the values and vision of this young person. By now, you can see that futuring is not very mysterious or difficult, but it requires thought and a little time.

Now that you have examples of two visions of the future, it is time to start thinking about what you want to achieve with your own vision of the future. I think you will agree that the future is about change, but how much change do you want? As you develop your own visions of your future, are you playing out your life as you already see it, or are you creating a new life? Is your future about making your present world nicer, or about completely changing your world? Or is it something in between?

You can build several different visions of your future, then choose which vision is going to be yours. When you are satisfied that you have the right vision, you are ready to start developing strategies to achieve that vision, which we will do in the next chapter.

CHAPTER 16

Strategies to Achieve
Your Vision

CONCEPT

A strategy is simply a way to do something—but you must decide which ways are *best* for you to achieve each component of your vision.

People associate strategies with war, sports, chess, and other forms of competition, but a strategy is simply a way to do something. In the last chapter, you considered several questions. Where do you want your life to go? Why do you need a vision? What is your vision? This chapter is about "How?" How you will achieve your vision of the future. How you will deal with the high-probability, high-impact events in your life. That is where strategies become important.

A STRATEGY IS "HOW"

Remember, in the last chapter we compared a vision to a vacation. First you pick a destination—Paris, for example. Once you have picked a destination, how are you going to get there? Will you fly, drive, take a train or a boat, or find some other way to get to Paris? *How* you get there is your strategy. If you are starting from another continent, your strategy may involve an airline, a train, a bus, and a taxi—multiple strategies.

In many cases, you will be looking at more than one plausible strategy. That is important. You will want to look at several strategies for each situation, because you will want to find the best strategy or combination of strategies. You want to find the strategy that fits the situation and fits you. The part about "fits you" is important, because you must actually *do* the strategy to make it work. If you select a strategy that requires you to be outspoken or even belligerent on your own behalf but is something you cannot really do, then it is the wrong strategy for you. You must find the strategies that work for you.

In this chapter, you are going to start by looking at strategies for two areas. The first will be strategies to achieve your vision for your life ten years from now. Figure 16.1 offers an example of a worksheet from twenty-year-old Jan, whose strategies deal directly with the vision described in the previous chapter.

	Strategies to achieve your goals and your vision
Activities	MFA U of Iowa—Do research in low-wage jobs in controversial industries (start with publishing and distribution) Write constantly for publication. Learn distribution and promotion in book industry
Finances	Live frugally on spouse income until royalties and paid articles start
Health	Focus on good health, diet, exercise
Housing	North Bay, small home near markets, schools. Office in home
Social	Marry after college (22) or grad school (24), first child at 30. Close family relationships, parents and siblings
Transportation	Mostly bicycle, one family car, prefer electric, buy new and own min ten years

Figure 16.1 - Jan's strategies to achieve the goals of the vision worksheet.

The strategies above are intended to achieve Jan's vision for the next ten years. Jan wants to be a writer, so the strategy is to seek a graduate degree in writing (Master of Fine Arts) in a very high quality graduate program. In order to have something to write about, Jan will follow the example of many successful authors and do research into how people work and live. Jan also intends to work in the publishing industry in order to learn about the industry. Each of these strategies is intended to prepare Jan for a career in writing.

Other strategies include a frugal lifestyle, a focus on maintaining good physical health, a practical home, a planned, close family, and a lifestyle that reflect Jan's values.

Jan's second worksheet, figure 16.2, addresses the high-impact, high-probability events commonly found in the young adult stage, the twenties.

	Strategies to deal with high-impact events
Activities	Graduate college, enter grad school, then create my own job writing. Work at low-pay jobs as research for books, stories, and articles.
Finances	Careful management of funds, taxes, insurance, investments. Avoid debt other than mortgage. Health and life insurance from spouse employer. Spouse is breadwinner until my writing starts selling.
Health	Work to stay healthy, avoid risky behaviors or situations.
Housing	Carefully select home to raise family and retire in. Good area, North Bay, close to market and schools.
Social	Marry after graduation, build new social circles but retain ties, wait till 30 for first child, network, keep close family ties.
Transportation	Walk or bicycle locally. Commute to city by ferry. Small car for longer trips, hopefully electric. Overseas travel when financially feasible.

Figure 16.2 - Jan's worksheet of strategies to deal with high-impact events that may occur during this life stage.

There is some overlap between the two worksheets, but that should be expected. Again, there is nothing dramatic in these strategies other than Jan keeping options open for the timing of a marriage. Yet Jan has clearly thought about the future and has prepared a number of strategies that reflect not only goals and events, but also personal values. These worksheets do not consider wild card events like the earthquakes that occasionally shake the San Francisco area, but those strategies will be explored in another chapter with Jan's contingency plan. Below is Jan's long-term worksheet of strategies to achieve goals and a vision through age seventy-five.

	Strategies to achieve your goals and your vision to age seventy-five
Activities	Spouse will retire by 70 so we can travel world. Will keep writing as long as I can.
Finances	Be wise with money, avoid debt other than mortgage, and pay off before retirement. Save and invest for life and retirement. Invest, don't lose! Continue to generate income streams.
Health	Focus on good health, diet, exercise. Protect vision, hearing, skin, and joints for long life. If sick or injured, work hard for fast, full recovery. Maintain living will and instructions to physicians and family.
Housing	Home in North Bay area, large enough to raise family but small enough to retire in. Office in home. Stay aware of earthquake and tsunami risks.
Social	Base our life in one place so family HQ stays same. Build social base here that will be constant throughout life. Continue to build friendships throughout life.
Transportation	Emphasis on walking, bicycles, and green cars or public transport. Develop mobility and transport alternatives in case of disability or frailty.

Figure 16.3 - Jan's worksheet of strategies to deal with high-impact events up to age seventy-five.

Look at these three sets of strategies, starting with activities. Jan has plans to enroll in a writing program at a very good graduate school, a strategy that should provide a good start to a writing career. This is accompanied by a strategy to conduct research and establish a career as an independent writer. Writing is viewed as a small, in-home business. Jan plans to continue the writing career even past retirement age. However, what if Jan has an opportunity to become a career editor in a San Francisco publishing firm? That is a decision Jan can make on its own merits at that time but does not really change the overall plan for a lifetime of writing.

In figure 16.3, notice that Jan has a different approach to housing compared to many in the United States. Jan will invest in a home and an area for life. This strategy impacts the financial domain because the mortgage will be paid off before retirement. The social domain is also affected, as Jan will maintain a long-term social network, which many people lose whenever they sell a home and move to a different area.

How will you develop your own strategies? What do you need to know? Think of war and sport metaphors. Are you attacking or defending? The strategies and tactics will be different, depending on what you want to achieve.

Start with defense. First, know what is happening, and try not to be surprised by events. That is one of the big reasons you are exploring the future—so you will have some idea what is coming next and be prepared to deal with it.

Look at the list of high-impact events in chapter 6. At the top of the list, the events that have the greatest impact in most people's lives are the deaths of close family members. Child, spouse, sibling, parent. The death of a child is tragic and can seldom be anticipated unless a long illness is involved. But many children die of accidents or injuries. The defensive strategy is to reduce the possibility of such an accident occurring. You cannot keep children in a bubble, but you can be involved in and aware of your children's lives. You can also actively work toward keeping your child, your spouse, and yourself healthy. Good diet, hygiene, and exercise are great starting points for the whole family.

Parents are a different situation. As they grow older, the risk of serious illness or death increases. Again, awareness and involvement are good strategies. Awareness reduces the likelihood of a surprise. Involvement can help reduce the risk of an avoidable death.

SOME SIMPLE STRATEGIES

Now that you are thinking about strategies, here are a few to help you get started. I am very careful in my workshops to not give advice on how to run your life. I'm qualified to help you learn how to use futures methods, but I'm not qualified to give advice on how you should live your life! However, here are a few brief strategies that have been recommended by others, and you may find some of them helpful.

	Simple strategies
Activities	Educate yourself, then do something you enjoy!
Finances	Don't lose money!
Health	Don't get sick.
Housing	A home that fits you.
Social	Nurture good relationships.
Transportation	Have alternatives.

Figure 16.4 - A few very brief strategies for your personal domains.

Look at each of these strategies more closely. A quick phrase is effective for making a point, but some of these need a little explanation.

Activities: Educate yourself, then do something you enjoy!

That is a pretty simple strategy. Educate yourself about everything you can, including how the world around you works. Education will also help you do something you enjoy. This relates primarily to you work or career, but includes all your activities. Your working life may last fifty years or more, so doing something that you enjoy will make that time much more interesting. Many people get trapped in jobs that they hate or at least dislike enough to be unhappy. If you are starting a career, try to do something you will enjoy. If you are already working and hate your work, find a way to make a change to something you like as soon as you reasonably can. Also, it is never too early to think about a backup or second career—something you might enjoy more than being fully retired. Keep in mind that life expectancies are already increasing. Research in medical and biological sciences will probably introduce breakthroughs that will keep people healthier and living longer. Possibly much longer.

No matter what age you are now, if you want to make a change in your life, the education strategy still applies. I went back to school when I was in my sixties and changed my life. Having a very supportive wife helped!

Finances: Do not lose money!

Wherever you are in this world, whatever your age or financial status, if you have some money, there will be people who try to take it away from you. Some will be legitimate businesses who are simply trying to sell you their products. Individuals may threaten you with violence in order to get your money. There will be all sorts of schemes, risks, and gambles that are intended to separate you from your money. *Educate* yourself about money, taxes, insurance, investments, and scams. Handle your money wisely and do not lose any of it. One other financial strategy: Keep some wiggle room! Be careful of your financial commitments, because they can lock you in to bad situations. If you are in debt, losing a job can be a disaster, but you can also be locked into a job that you hate simply because you cannot afford to make a change.

Health: Do not get sick!

I understand that people do not get sick on purpose, but most of us could do more to prevent illness. Good hygiene, washing your hands, bathing, brushing your teeth, and flossing are a good start. A healthy diet is also important, because a bad diet can cause health problems, such as Type II diabetes. Inhaling smoke from cigarettes or inhaling pollutants or allergens from the air around you can make you sick. My wife developed bronchial infections due to industrial chemicals in the air at a previous home, so we moved. Her health returned, and both of us found that our allergy problems improved significantly.

There are a lot of ways to get sick or damage your body, and once your body is damaged, it takes time to heal. Unfortunately, some illnesses are permanent. With many illnesses or injuries, once you have the condition, it is not easy to recover. The best strategy is to do *everything* you can to avoid illness or injury. This is true regardless of age. Young people take more physical risks; older people are more vulnerable to disease or injury. In between these age groups, people get out of shape and ignore health problems or injuries that accumulate gradually.

Housing: Decide what you need, what you want, and what the difference is.

Your home is where you live, whether it is an apartment, a mud hut, a tent, a bungalow, or a McMansion. Some people prefer to live a nomadic life, so housing is temporary.

So what is your housing strategy? Your home may be where you want to raise a family and eventually retire. You may consider your home an investment, a place with land, or a showplace. If you are frail, home may be an assisted living facility where you live to receive some help with life.

If you have a young family, your strategy will be different from what it will be if you are elderly and need help. Your home and its location should meet the needs that are important to you. When your needs change, you can change your home, either through remodeling or moving to a different home.

Social: Nurture good relationships.

Good relationships are worth nurturing. Love, friendship, and respect are valuable, because humans are social animals. Here you will be considering a very general strategy of having people in your life on whom you can count in some way.

Your family and a few close friends will usually be your inner network, and these are the people whom you help or who help you through good times and difficult times. You will probably have a wider circle of friends with whom you can exchange thoughts, advice, and ideas, or maybe just an occasional joke through your email. Beyond those circles will be the people you know through school or work or just see frequently. One thing to remember is that any time you move to a different area, you will change social circles. You will leave familiar social circles and establish new circles. That is hard for some people and should be considered before making a change.

Transportation: Have alternatives.

If the car does not start, the bus does not come, the trainmen are on strike, or your flight is cancelled, what do you do? Do you have strategies to deal with those situations? Sometimes the most important strategy is to clear away the stress—because there is no convenient time for any of those problems—and then deal with the problem. Sometimes you will have to accept what you cannot change; that, too, is a strategy.

If your commute to work is way too long, what is your strategy for change? Even if your strategy will not immediately eliminate your commute, knowing that there will be a change in the future may make the daily trips more tolerable.

When you get older, you may have to stop driving or using mass transit. You will need a strategy that will help you get to the market or the doctor's office (or bring them to you). If you become sick or disabled, will caregivers come to your home? What are your alternatives?

By simply thinking ahead about potential problems, sometimes years ahead, you have time to develop or recognize workable strategies. That is part of the value of developing a long-term perspective.

Those are all simple situations and simple strategies, but they illustrate what you have been thinking about in this chapter. Now that you know what you want your future to be and have strategies to achieve that future, the next chapter will lead you through the process of creating an action plan for the next ten years of your life.

CHAPTER 17

Creating Your Action Plan

CONCEPT

STRATEGIES must be executed in a sequence of steps over time. The action plan develops the sequence of steps for each strategy then maps out the time period for executing that strategy. Some strategies may be accomplished quickly, and others will take the entire time period for the plan.

The action plan is where you turn your strategies into actions, then map them out for the next ten years. It is like a long-term to-do list for each strategy. Look back at your vision and your strategies to remind yourself what you want to achieve and how you want to achieve it. What actions must you take over the next ten years to achieve your vision? For each strategy that you have developed, what is the first step, and the next, and the next?

STRATEGIES IN SEQUENCES

You do not have to build a lot of detail into your strategic plan. In your strategies, you have already decided what you have to do to achieve your future. Therefore, in your strategic plan, you are deciding when you are going to take each step to execute your strategies. Following is a list of strategies that Jan compiled:

	Strategies over the next ten years
Activities School Career Travel Sport, hobbies Religion	Best available MFA program Research and write anything and everything—Get agent, publishers Work in areas of research Book tours
Finances Income Expense Financing Insurance	Book and article sales, research job income School Grad school Married Grants, scholarship Thru parents until married, then through spouse
Health Activities Maintenance	Daily, weekly exercise and hygiene, diet Vaccinations, five-year exam, monitor
Housing	Shared apt. at school When married, rent until we can own
Social	Stay close to family and friends Network in writing, publishing circles
Transportation Local Other	Bike, walk Mass transit

Figure 17.1 - Jan's summary of strategies for the next ten years.

Jan's first strategy is "Best available MFA program." That will start with selecting schools for application and conclude with graduation. The steps from beginning to end will include:

- Pick five best MFA schools in United States and complete applications
- From acceptances, pick first choice and accept. Apply for funding.
- Enroll, find housing, and start classes
- Complete program and graduate

Other steps may appear during the process, but these are enough steps for strategic planning. The next step is to determine when each step must be completed and to insert the steps into your action plan. In the case of applying for graduate schools, there will probably be a detailed set of deadlines that must be met. Your action plan does not support that much detail, so you will probably want to build specific timelines or calendars for different projects.

Make a list of steps for each of your strategies, and decide when each step needs to be accomplished. Then, add the strategy steps to your action plan.

YOUR ACTION PLAN

Below is Jan's action plan, starting during age twenty-one and ending during age thirty. The worksheet is based on calendar years to keep the chart simple. There are entries only where an action is to be taken during that year. In Jan's plan, the focus is on a writing career, and you can see a clear vision of getting a very good start with a graduate degree in creative writing from a good school, then slowly building a career on a solid foundation.

Calendar year	Actions to be taken each year
Year One 2010 **Activities** **Finances** **Health** **Housing** **Social** **Transportation**	Prepare and submit apps to MFA grad schools
Year Two 2011 **Activities** **Finances** **Health** **Housing** **Social** **Transportation**	Graduate from college, enter grad school. Iowa! Apply for financial aid or grant Rent near campus

Year Three 2012 **Activities** **Finances** **Health** **Housing** **Social** **Transportation**	Complete first year grad school Apply for financial aid or grant Rent near campus
Year Four 2013 **Activities** **Finances** **Health** **Housing** **Social** **Transportation**	Complete MFA, graduate. Apply for work at San Francisco publishers. Write! Get health insurance Two BR rental in North Bay—one room for office Wedding!!! Honeymoon! Sell one car
Year Five 2014 **Activities** **Finances** **Health** **Housing** **Social** **Transportation**	Complete manuscript; find an agent, SF or NY. Rewrite Looking for a house
Year Six 2015 **Activities** **Finances** **Health** **Housing** **Social** **Transportation**	Promote first book, travel, signings, speaking. Write! Living in our own home in North Bay. Have a permanent office with view Electrics are hot and reliable. Buy our first new car.
Year Seven 2016 **Activities** **Finances** **Health** **Housing** **Social** **Transportation**	Submit manuscript for book two Rewrite

CREATING YOUR ACTION PLAN

Year Eight 2017 **Activities** **Finances** **Health** **Housing** **Social** **Transportation**	Another book tour. Experience makes a difference! Writing. Investing most royalty income. CDs, long treasuries, stripped treasuries Meeting friends from earlier tour!
Year Nine 2018 **Activities** **Finances** **Health** **Housing** **Social** **Transportation**	Submit manuscript for book three. Rewrite Investing most royalty income. CDs, long treasuries, stripped treasuries
Year Ten 2019 **Activities** **Finances** **Health** **Housing** **Social** **Transportation**	Another book tour. Writing has jelled into real enterprise. Hire assistant Between spouse 401K and royalty investments, retirement is secure. Still doing same workout, healthy diet, and hygiene! Minor remodel and paint. Start a family! All parents in midfifties.

Figure 17.2 - Jan's strategic plan for the next ten years.
Simple and to the point.

As you can see from Jan's worksheet, the personal strategic plan can be simple and straightforward. For the most part, you can follow the strategies that you devised earlier, laying the steps out over ten years, leaving enough time to accomplish one step before moving on to the next. The six domains listed under each year on the worksheet serve as guides, but you do not have to write anything in unless there is something you want to accomplish in that domain in that year. Notice that in Jan's plan, there are no actions listed for the health domain until the last year. That is because there is nothing new. The routine is already established. On the other hand, the steps toward preparing for and establishing a writing career are spelled out for each year.

You can put as much or as little detail into your plan as you choose. It is your plan, and the level of detail is up to you. The amount of detail in Jan's plan is adequate to achieve the vision that was prepared earlier. When you

182 It's Your Future

progress through the plan each year, you will be able to think in more detail about what you want to do that year. You may be ahead of the plan or behind the plan, so you can adjust to the realities of your life each year.

Again, look at Jan's plan. The plan says, "Write!" It says nothing about what to write. Just "Write!" Jan may plot out each book in great detail, then write the book that year, but none of that has to be part of the strategic plan. Yet, if Jan has a plan for a series of books and wants to write in the proposed titles for every book instead of book numbers, that is fine. These are all details that are left up to you.

But what happens if the plan is not working? What if, after several years of writing, Jan realizes that this part of the plan is not succeeding? Jan has not written alternatives or a decision date into the plan, but there obviously must be alternatives. Jan can keep on writing and trying to get published; seek a career in publishing; or use the qualifications and credentials in the MFA to teach university students to write.

Then it is time to rewrite the plan. The same applies to your plan. If you see that your plan is not in synch with reality, you can change or rewrite your plan at any time.

BACKCASTING

Sometimes people have trouble deciding which actions to take and when to take them. They start working on their plan with enthusiasm, then become bogged down. They get into difficulty developing the sequences of the actions. The first steps are easy, but identifying the tasks and their sequence gets harder.

Futurists have a technique for solving that problem. It is called "Backcasting."

The idea is really simple. Start in the future and work backward, because once you are in the future, you know how you got there! Does that sound logical and crazy at the same time? The funny thing is, it works. Here is how.

You will need a quiet place where you can relax, close your eyes, and think about your future. Think about ten years from now, when you are actually living in the future of your vision. You may start taking your mind into the future by thinking of one of your favorite activities, thinking how that activity will change for you over ten years. Then visualize yourself in that activity ten years from now. Once your mind is in the future, look around at your life. See how much things have changed to bring you to this future. Now, ask yourself,

"What was the last thing I had to accomplish to make my vision complete? What did I have to accomplish before that? And before that?" Write those steps down, from the future to the present, and that will give you a sequence of events that you can follow with your strategic plan; in following the steps, however, you will be going from the present toward the future.

The sequence is what you are looking for. Whether you work out the sequence of tasks going backward or forward, once you have a sequence, working out the timing will be easy.

Backcasting sounded crazy to me before I tried it, but it worked. Many people from workshops and mini-workshops have told me that they were skeptical but that backcasting, worked for them as well. It is worth a try!

Now you have a plan for your future! This plan is pretty important, so you should probably take a few minutes to analyze your plan using a few tools that futurists find valuable. In the next chapter you will search through your plan to expose gaps, vulnerabilities, or unintended consequences.

CHAPTER 18

Analyzing Your Plan

CONCEPT

IT is always a good idea to review your work. Several tools from strategic planning are available to help you analyze your plan and strengthen it.

Strategic planning includes a number of techniques to test the strategic plan as it is being constructed or to critique the plan after is has been written. You are working on a personal scale, so the three techniques introduced here should be sufficient to analyze your plan and provide an opportunity to become familiar with these tools. The explanations and examples are simplified, but the concepts are just as valid in your personal life as they are in an organization of any size.

VULNERABILITY ANALYSIS

What event or events could possibly happen to cause your life as you know it to crash?

In recent years, families have been driven to destitution and worse by forces apparently out of their control. Homes lost to foreclosures in the mortgage crisis. Life savings lost to Ponzi schemes. Homes and belongings lost to fires, storms, earthquakes, and floods.

For many people, these events hit them when they were vulnerable. Some knew that they were taking chances, but others had no idea that their entire way of life was at risk. Think of your life, for a moment, as a table with six legs, your six domains. How many legs can you lose before your table (and your way of life) falls down? Which domains are most critical, and which domains are vulnerable? What can you do to reduce the vulnerabilities and the risk of collapse?

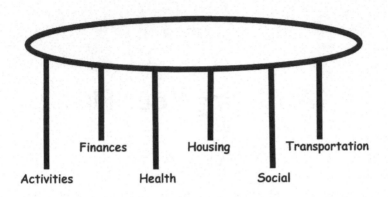

Figure 18.1 - A six-legged table will probably fall if
any three legs are removed.

What would it take to knock you down? These are the questions to ask and answer in the vulnerability analysis. Some people are more emotionally vulnerable than others are, which makes them more vulnerable to any crisis. The reverse is that some people are emotionally stronger than others are and will struggle through and survive nearly any catastrophe. That personal strength or vulnerability may be a seventh leg on the table for some people, but we will focus on your personal domains.

Following is an example of a vulnerability analysis for twenty-year-old Jan.

	Vulnerabilities	Risk reduction
Activities	Loss of spouse's job Writing career fails to develop	Increase Jan's income Teach or full-time work
Finances	Loss of income and insurance	Second income and Savings Alternate insurance
Health	Serious illness or injury, self or spouse	Insurance Good health, physical condition
Housing	Earthquake, tsunami Wildfires Over-mortgaged	Home not near waterfront Home not in forested area Large down payment, fixed rate Insurance
Social	Divorce Death of spouse or family member	Always keep our relationship first Insurance
Transportation	Loss of mobility	Alternative transport Insurance

Figure 18.2 - Jan's vulnerability analysis.

Jan has uncovered some important vulnerabilities, including risks to a home that is still five years in the future! Shorter term (two to four years away) is the economic risk if Jan's spouse, the only wage-earner for the first few years of their marriage, becomes unemployed. This reflects long-term thinking, which is one of the goals of learning personal strategic planning. In the risk reduction column, Jan may have to think about working at something that would provide a backup income if needed. In other areas, insurance provides an alternative.

In most cases, this young couple could survive one of these events, but a second event could be very damaging. An associated problem is that some-times negative events are like dominoes. One event causes another, which triggers a third. For example, a serious injury or illness might cause the loss of a job, which in turn takes away both income and insurance, which creates so many problems that bankruptcy or divorce may follow.

This cascading of overwhelming events is also seen among older people when an event like a stroke makes an individual dependent on a caregiver. If that caregiver is a spouse, that extra burden may be more than the spouse (or the marriage) can handle. In the meantime, the stroke victim has therapy, doctor appointments, and prescriptions, yet is unable to drive, placing addi-tional stress and burden on the caregiving spouse. If the couple has a supportive network of family and friends who will help carry the burden, they may get through, but they may not. Often the caregiver becomes ill from the long overload burden.

On the other hand, seeing the risks or vulnerabilities well in advance may strengthen your strategic plan. For example, Jan saw the risk of being over-mortgaged and proposed making a larger down payment. That may mean that the young couple will rent longer while they save for a larger down payment, but they will reduce the risk of losing their home. Jan also recognized the risks of living too close to a shoreline or to a wilderness. The couple will have several years to explore alternatives before they purchase their home, but they are already recognizing how to limit their exposure to risk.

This is the value of vulnerability analysis. The process uncovers areas where risks exist; then it shows how the risks exist side by side with other vulnerabili-ties that could combine to become a personal disaster. Most importantly, the analysis shows where it is imperative to reduce the risk or identify solutions to deal with the potential problems. Those solutions may become part of your contingency plan, which is a key element of your strategic plan.

GAP ANALYSIS

Sometimes an idea sounds really good, but for one reason or another, it will not work. This is where "I want" meets "I can."

"Let's ride a raft down the river!" But you do not have a raft. "Let's take a vacation!" But there is no money in the bank. There is a gap between the plan and reality. When businesses find gaps in their strategic plans, the gaps often relate to funds. The plan calls for a project that requires money, but no funds are available. Jan's plan for year six includes buying a new home. If the rest of the plan succeeds and there is sufficient royalty income, then a mortgage and new home should be workable. But, if there is little or no income from writing, this may be a gap.

In the worksheet below, Jan has identified a potential gap in the vision and has corrected it in the action plan.

	Plan	Potential gap	Possible solution
Activities			
Finances	Grad school	Tuition, books	Delay marriage, parents offered to provide
Health			
Housing	Housing during grad school	Rent	Delay marriage, parents will provide. Dorm?
Social	Marriage after college	Separation during grad school	Delay marriage till after grad school
Transportation			

Figure 18.3 - Jan's example of gap analysis.

CLOSING THE GAPS

Jan's vision considered getting married after graduating from the university. After considering the two-year separation and the costs of grad school, delaying the marriage seemed like a good solution. Both sets of parents had encouraged delaying marriage until after grad school, but only during the process of creating a strategic plan did Jan recognize the wisdom in their advice. Similar logic may have applied to starting a family, resulting in the couple deciding to wait until they were thirty to have their first child. By then, they should be financially stable, and both careers should be on track before taking on more responsibility.

Gap analysis helps to close the gap between what you want to do and what you can successfully accomplish.

Unintended Consequences

Analysis of the personal strategic plan created by our twenty-year-old student revealed that strategies and actions can result in unintended consequences. There is a folk law, something like Murphy's Law, which says that if people (or governments) take action, there will be unanticipated or unintended consequences. You should be aware of this law before you put your action plan into effect. Here is why.

In the example of gap analysis, Jan realized that marriage after college would have some unintended consequences. This suggests that there is value in re-reading your vision, your strategies, and your plans, constantly asking yourself, "If I do this, what are the consequences? What do I intend, and what may happen that I don't intend to happen?"

A good tool for revealing unintended consequences is the personal futures wheel, which starts with your six domains. This encourages you to consider impacts in each domain.

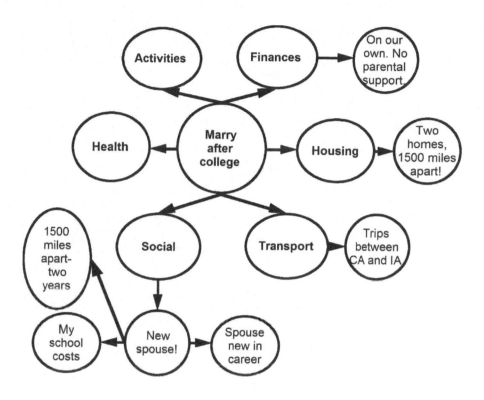

Figure 18.4 - Jan's analysis showing consequences
of marriage after graduation.

Jan used the futures wheel to look at the consequences of marrying right
after graduation from the university and realized that there would be substan-
tial strains on the new marriage. A second analysis looked at the consequences
of delaying marriage until completion of graduate school.

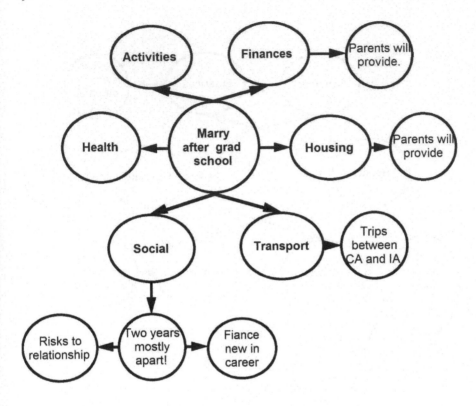

Figure 18.5 - Jan's analysis of marriage after grad school.

Sometimes the unintended effects will be positive, and sometimes they will be negative. The negatives are probably what you will be most concerned about. However, if there are positive consequences, it is best to know in advance so you can give yourself credit and not be surprised when they occur.

This is a technique that you can use anywhere in your life or career as you ponder a decision; before you act, ask yourself, "What are the unintended consequences?"

Now that you have analyzed your action plan, you are ready for the final step in your strategic plan: contingency planning, which is the next chapter.

CHAPTER 19

Wild Cards and Contingency Planning

CONCEPTS

LOW-probability events that would have a big impact on your life are important to consider and prepare for. Identify possible events, then develop strategies and plans for dealing with each.

In previous chapters, I have referred several times to wild cards. In this chapter, you will finally have the chance to explore and deal with them. These are all of the low-probability, high-impact events in your future that are possible but not plausible or probable. Could happen, but not likely.

In this chapter, you will identify your potential wild card events, then make a plan to deal with each event if and when it occurs.

You might call this "If... then" planning. *If* this event happens, *then* these are the actions that you will take.

I have had a personal wild card for over twenty years. Hurricanes. We live on the Gulf Coast of Texas, about thirty miles inland, so we do not have to worry about the storm surge, but we do have to be concerned about wind and rain. We have a contingency plan for hurricanes. It is very simple. When hurricane season opens in June, we start paying attention to weather forecasts, particularly if a tropical storm or hurricane appears to be forming. When one forms, we watch its projected path. If Brownsville is in the path, we start making early preparations. If the storm still appears headed our way two days before landfall, we cover the windows with plywood and turn off the power and water. We next move everything important to higher shelves in case of high water. Then we pack the car and leave town, usually to stay with relatives who live about two hundred miles inland.

That is one example of a personal contingency plan. We also have a backup plan in case we cannot leave home before the storm arrives. In the summer of 2008, we used both plans. Having a plan gave us confidence. Some neighbors had plans and experience with hurricanes, but many others had no idea what actions to take to prevent loss or injury.

WILD CARDS

This is a good point to review potential wild cards in your own life. If high-impact, low-probability events do not just pop into your mind, look back at chapter 6. There is a list of life-changing events as well as a page of events for your stage of life that may give you some ideas.

Below are some events from those two lists that Jan listed before filling out a contingency plan.

	Wild Card Events (Hi Impact, Lo Probability) For the Young Adult stage	Life-Change events
Activities	Extreme success Extreme failure	Fired from work Retirement
Financial	Extreme success Extreme failure	Investment or credit problems Foreclosure
Health	Extreme depression, Suicide Unplanned pregnancy	Major injury or illness
Housing	Major (unexpected) relocation Loss of home	
Social	Multiple family deaths or injuries Multiple birth (triplets or more)	Death of family member or close friend Divorce of parents Divorce
Transportation	Public transport accident Buy a Ferrari!	

Figure 19.1 - Jan's list of wild cards for the young adult stage
and life-change events.

One characteristic of wild cards is that people (futurists included) tend to think first of negative wild cards—disasters. Yet, there are a lot of positive, happy wild cards available. Notice that Jan listed "extreme success" in the activities and financial domains, and "buy a Ferrari" in the transportation domain. The point here is to push yourself to think of positive as well as negative events.

This brings up another point that you should be aware of, which futurists call "cascading wild cards." This happens when the occurrence of one wild card causes other wild cards to take place. In Jan's case, extreme career success could lead to extreme financial success, which might lead to buying a Ferrari. The same can happen on the negative side. An illness or injury causes temporary disability that results in the loss of a job, which leads to loss of insurance, which in turn causes the individual's financial ruin.

Knowing about this potential chain reaction in advance will allow you to build a contingency plan that will deal with this domino effect.

Your Contingency Plan

One of the benefits of contingency planning is that you are encouraged to think about events before they happen and then think about how you can get through that event. This is an opportunity to confront your fears and think about how you would actually manage those fears if a negative event actually occurred.

This is also a good time to recognize that there *will* be some negative, high-impact events in your life. If you accept that fact, you can then think about the ways you can react or respond to different events. Hopefully, if you make a contingency plan for an event, you will take the opportunity to think through how you will respond to that event, step by step. That process of developing a plan to deal with an event may also help to reduce your fears of the event.

At the same time, there will probably be some *positive* high-impact events in your life, and you can make contingency plans to deal with those as well. These should be easier to plan for because these are the events that people daydream about!

It may help you to think about your contingency plans if you remember that this is similar to simulator training; the way that pilots, drivers, astronauts, and many other people are trained. Simulator training presents potential high-impact events (literally, in some cases) and requires the pilot, driver, or operator to respond with pre-tested strategies. By rehearsing their responses to adverse or difficult situations, these people are prepared for those events with appropriate responses when the event actually occurs. Contingency plans help you develop successful strategies to deal with high impact events that may occur in your life and your future.

The chart below shows what Jan picked from the list above, then added a few more unlikely but possible events over the next ten years. It is a formidable list for a twenty year old!

	Potential High-impact Event	Contingency Plan: Actions to take
Activities	Unable to develop writing career Extreme success	Change career to teaching or work in publishing. Reinvest to expand research and production
Finances	Parents can't fund grad school	Student grant, loan, part-time work or full-time work and part-time school Change grad school to live at home
Health	Serious illness or injury	Do everything possible to return to 100 percent health Prepare Living Will, DNR, Instructions
Housing	Bay Area earthquake or other disaster	Stay alive! Minimize risk. Have home prepared for emergency (food, water, candles, batteries, radio) or evacuation (documents)
Social	Family member death or serious illness Marriage fails	Separate emotion from action. Protect self. Act.
Transportation	Public transit or ferry failure	Communicate. If in city, stay with friend if necessary.

Figure 19.2 - Jan's contingency plan for the next ten years.

Obviously, the contingency plans shown here are simply the headlines. In some cases, the headline may be sufficient, and more detailed planning will take place as an event becomes an approaching reality. For example, if Jan's writing career is not succeeding, there should be time to prepare to change careers.

On the other hand, if an earthquake hits, there is no time for preparation, so a detailed plan with alternatives should be prepared in advance. That plan should consider where each person (Jan and spouse) might be at the time of the earthquake and how they will communicate or seek shelter if necessary. The futures wheel may be helpful in creating this plan as well.

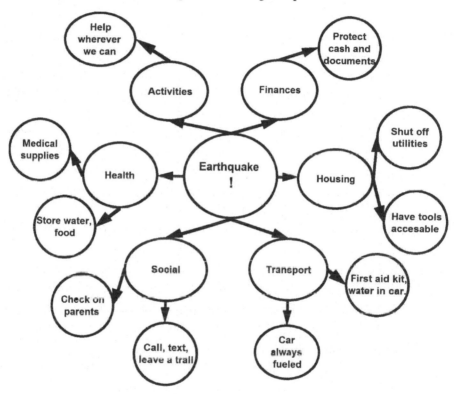

Figure 19.3 - Jan starts planning with a futures wheel.

In the example above, Jan has started planning for an earthquake using the futures wheel. This example could grow substantially as more situations come to mind and more detail is needed.

In your own plan, you should consider how you would deal with a very serious injury or death of a spouse. In addition, it may be helpful to talk to your parents and your spouse's parents to learn what plans they have for injury or death of a spouse. What part might you play in those plans, if any?

In the early 1960s, Herman Kahn wrote a book about the possibilities of nuclear war titled, *Thinking the Unthinkable*. The existence of the book forced people to think about nuclear war, a subject that most people wanted to avoid considering.

Thinking the unthinkable is a good title for thinking about negative wild cards, because when you think about the future, it is necessary to consider the unpleasant possibilities. These are the events that most people avoid discussing. Death. Dementia. Serious illness or injury. Financial ruin. Any of these for yourself, your spouse, a child, a parent, or anyone close to you. Not fun stuff, but you cannot just walk around it and hope it never happens, because some unpleasant events will happen.

People die, get seriously ill, or suffer terrible injuries. It will almost certainly happen in your family sometime. The point is that by thinking about the unthinkable events in your life, you can prepare to deal with such things. If you avoid considering these events, the initial trauma of the event may make outcomes worse than they need to be.

What can you do? Make a will. Sign a DNR or instructions to physicians even if you are young. Talk with your spouse about negative events so that you each know what the other wants in the event of any unthinkable event, and think about how you can deal with these events. Talk about them and get them out in the open if only to help reduce the shock value if one of these events happens. Finally, think about what must be done to deal with these events and add then to your contingency plan.

Then think about your positive wild cards! One advantage of the positive wild cards is that they carry less risk of immediate depression. However, they can seem to spin your world out of control, so it is a good idea to have a contingency plan.

Jan also wrote out a contingency plan to deal with events that may occur during later stages of life.

	Potential High-impact Event	Contingency Plan: Actions to take
Activities	Loss of job (self or spouse) Extreme career success	Consult; network; keep resume updated Retain financial/tax/legal advisor. Add researcher(s)
Finances	Economic crisis Extreme financial success Extreme long life	Minimize impact. Invest conservatively—don't lose principle! Avoid debt. Retain financial/tax/legal advisor. Maximize investment safety of principle and earnings. Protect financial reserves. Maintain income
Health	Serious illness or injury Decline of vision, hearing, mental, etc. Alzheimer's Extreme long life	Do everything possible to return to 100 percent health Prepare Living Will, DNR, Instructions Aggressively fight to retain all senses and abilities Know what choices are for care at home or facility Stay physically and mentally healthy
Housing	May have to move for care	Long-term care insurance
Social	Deaths, divorce, disasters of family members	Monitor, anticipate, and prepare for each person
Transportation	Cannot drive	Have alternative drivers, transport, or communication for short or long term.

Figure 19.4 - Jan's contingency plan for late life.

Notice that Jan has included extreme long life as a wild card. This is a wild card that could soon become a plausible event for more and more people. General awareness of healthy lifestyles accompanied by a few breakthroughs in biological and medical sciences could extend human life spans substantially in the next few decades. Contingency plans for the fifty-year future are probably premature for Jan, and they will be changed over time, but it is good to think ahead. Changing a plan is okay, and it is easier to make changes than to start from scratch. The real benefit comes from thinking about the possibilities. In thinking about these possibilities and working out contingency plans, you are starting to shape your future. In these cases, you may be thinking through events that you fear or dread. You may find, as many have before you, that the fear of some events is worse than the event itself, and that some preparation can greatly reduce the psychological impacts of these events.

The contingency plan is the last document in your strategic plan. If you have been using the *Personal Futures Workbook* or writing out a plan as you read this, your personal strategic plan is now complete. In the next chapter, you will look at your life with a plan and will learn how to use and maintain your plan most effectively.

CHAPTER 20

Living With Your Plan

CONCEPT

FIRST, live your plan. Follow the plan you have created, yet feel free to change the plan at any time. Second, no matter how carefully you plan, the future is unlikely to follow your plan entirely. By having a plan, you are prepared to recognize change early in order to adjust your life and your plan to meet reality.

Congratulations! You have gone through the whole process of personal strategic planning. If you have been filling out the worksheets in the *Personal Futures Workbook,* you now have a written plan for the next ten years of your life. You have a detailed map to your future.

The whole purpose of this book is to encourage you to *think* about the future. *Your* future. Just reading this book is a start, but creating scenarios and a strategic plan are the big steps. The simple action of taking time to think about your future is the most important element in the futuring process. The thinking makes everything else work.

So, what is next?

LIVE YOUR PLAN!

Live your plan! It is that simple. Live the plan you have created. Follow your action plan and watch for results from the actions you take, but be patient. Remember, this is a ten-year plan. Some of the changes brought about by your plan may be disruptive, and some may involve change for other people who may resist until they understand the value to themselves of your plan. Year by year, continue with your plan and observe the results.

At the same time, keep your contingency plan up to date. You should review the plans for each of the events in your contingency plan and be prepared to add other events that may emerge as possible high-impact, low-probability events. For some events, like hurricanes, fires, and accidents, you may find checklists that others have prepared to deal with similar situations. Take advantage of all the experience and information that is available. For most events in your contingency plan, others have gone through the same experience and some of them have posted lists or written blogs with advice that you may be able to use.

Also, watch for change going on around you that you have not anticipated in your plans. There will be events or movement of forces that you did not or could not anticipate. Some events will not make any difference in your plan, but watch for signals that important change may be coming. In particular, watch for indications that one of your unexpected scenarios is starting to happen.

As you have read earlier, futurists focus on change, and you should too. Look for big change and little change. Monitor the world around you and your life in each of your domains. Watch for change in the lives of each of your stakeholders, and ask yourself how those changes may impact you. Then, try to anticipate whatever else is changing in your world so that you will not be surprised when an important event occurs.

On the other side of the equation, you can be the person who initiates change.

If you are young, your goals and desires may change over time. This is normal. When I was in my early twenties, I thought my career goal was to race sport cars. By my midtwenties, marriage and family became a dominant force, and a career in business became my new goal. In my sixties, I started reducing the size of my business, redirecting my goals to conducting research and writing about personal futures. The fact is that as our lives change or we achieve some goals, our desires or interests change and we seek new goals. The point is very simple. If your desires or goals change, change your plan.

When Your Vision Changes ...

Remember, your vision of your future is your destination, so your plan should be designed to take you to your vision. So, when your vision changes, change your plan.

When the world around you (STEEP forces) changes, adjust your plan. For example, if the world economy sinks (as it did in 2008, and as it will again in the future), or the reverse—if the economy soars, either event could affect your plans. If medical science succeeds in extending lifetimes dramatically, that could change your plans for the future. If the earth's climate swings from warming to cooling, and an ice age appears imminent, your future plans might change.

Similarly, your future may be impacted when your own world (personal domains) changes. A change of employers, a change in your health (or your spouse's health), or a change in your family (parenting a grandchild) may cause you to re-evaluate your plan and adjust it to meet your changing future. In any case, you will probably want to evaluate and update your plan every year.

Once again, that is what the future is all about—change. You can choose to fight it, roll with it, or embrace it, but your future is about change. Make the best of it!

CHAPTER 21

The Long-Term Perspective in Your Life and Your Career

CONCEPT

WHETHER you have just skimmed through this book or have gone through every exercise in the workbook, you should have absorbed some important concepts about long-term thinking. You should have some understanding about the future and how several key futures methods work. That knowledge can be valuable.

Now that you have seen how futures methods can give you a different perspective on your own life, what else can you do with what you have learned here? Actually, quite a bit.

SCALABILITY WORKS FOR YOU

You now have personal experience with the use of several important futures methods. These methods were all scaled down from corporate methods, which demonstrates their scalability. That scalability can work for you because these methods scale both ways. That means that your understanding and experience at the personal level with these methods can scale up to any level. In addition, now that you understand the concepts, you can use these methods on a daily basis to help you make personal or career decisions and to recognize early signals of change in your life, your career, and the world around you.

Relating events in daily life to forces and their impacts in the future are steps toward developing a long-term perspective.

Because these methods are scalable, everything that you have learned in this book can be applied to futuring or strategic planning in organizations of any size. A small business, government at any level, national organization, or international conglomerate—they all use these methods. The difference is the scale. The knowledge that you have gained in building your personal strategic plan will provide you insights into how scenarios and strategic planning are working in your career.

Do not misunderstand. You are not ready to be a professional futurist or to take charge of a corporation's strategic planning. But you do understand how the tools and the processes work in practical detail. You now have valuable knowledge to contribute.

THE LONG-TERM PERSPECTIVE

The ability to see events with a long-term perspective is a valuable trait. According to researchers James Kouzes and Barry Posner, having a long-term perspective is second only to honesty in sought-after leadership traits. This is a talent worth developing, and you have already learned the basic skills. I suspect that you are already asking, "How can I acquire a long-term perspective?"

Start simply. When faced with a decision, ask yourself, "What could happen? What is the worst case? What is the best case?" When you have good answers to those questions, you have put brackets around the future for that decision. You have narrowed the outcome to those outcomes that are plausible. That should help you with your decision.

Watch for the forces of change, internally and externally. Ask yourself questions, then find the answers. What is changing? What is causing that change? What is the driving force? How fast will it change? How far will this change go? Whom will this change impact, and how? To question a change, use the traditional questions that journalists have been asking since the beginning of journalism: Who? What? When? Where? Why? How? Then ask yourself what this change will look like in ten years or longer.

That probably sounds too simple, and it may be. The key step that is not mentioned above is the necessity of taking the time, after asking the questions, to develop and analyze the answers. In our fast-paced, multitasking world, that may well be the key to learning about the future—taking the time to think about it.

In addition to acquiring a long-term perspective for your own use, you may find value in helping others to acquire a long-term view in their lives and their careers. As a parent, your children will benefit from realizing that teen years and time spent gaining an education are a very small part of a life that may exceed 100 years. For educators, helping students to gain a perspective of time and understand the impact of an education on their long-term future may encourage more students to stay in school. For organizations of any type or size, there is clearly value in educating personnel at *all* levels in long-term thinking.

Above all else, this book is about you and *your* future. You now have the methods, the tools, and the knowledge to make your future a good one!

Appendix

BLANK WORKSHEETS BY CHAPTER
STAKEHOLDERS
CHAPTER 3

An Excel spreadsheet is available for free download at www.personalfutures.net or you can reconstruct this worksheet on your computer.

Family members: Ages and Stages

Year	Your age	Spouse age	Oldest child	Youngest child	Oldest parent	Others
Name						
2010						
2011						
2012						
2013						
2014						
2015						
2016						
2017						
2018						
2019						
2020						
2021						
2022						
2023						
2024						
2025						
2026						
2027						
2028						
2029						
2030						

Figure A.1

PERSONAL DOMAINS
CHAPTER 5
ACTIVITIES DOMAIN

Activities include school, training, self-improvement, work or career, religion, sports, hobbies, travel and the all other things you do. Some activities, such as addictions, are negative or destructive, and can also become driving forces.

Ages	0	10	20	30	40	50	60	70	80	90	100
Very Hi											
High											
Average											
Low											
Very Lo											

Figure A.2

What is your present level of satisfaction with your *activities* domain?

What would you like to change?

What would you have to do to initiate a change?

FINANCES DOMAIN

The finances domain includes everything that has to do with your finances, including your income, expenses, assets, liabilities, investments.

Ages	0	10	20	30	40	50	60	70	80	90	100
Very Hi											
High											
Average											
Low											
Very Lo											

Figure A.3

What is your present level of satisfaction with your *finances* domain?

What would you like to change?

What would you have to do to initiate a change?

Health Domain

The health domain includes everything related to your physical, emotional and mental health, for example your health status, conditions or diseases, medications, diet and exercise, medical care and personal care.

Ages	0	10	20	30	40	50	60	70	80	90	100
Very Hi											
High											
Average											
Low											
Very Lo											

Figure A.4

What is your present level of satisfaction with your *health* domain?

What would you like to change?

What would you have to do to initiate a change?

HOUSING DOMAIN

The housing domain includes your home, the neighborhood and community you live in, your country (including its political and economic systems) and the climate for your region of the world. If you live in (or expect to live in) a care facility, that is also part of your housing domain.

Ages	0	10	20	30	40	50	60	70	80	90	100
Very Hi											
High											
Average											
Low											
Very Lo											

Figure A.5

What is your present level of satisfaction with your *housing* domain?

What would you like to change?

What would you have to do to initiate a change?

Social Domain

The Social domain starts with family and closest friends, then expands outward to embrace your friends, co-workers, advisors and community. Sociology and other disciplines often use an illustration of nested circles to demonstrate some of these social relationships.

Ages	0	10	20	30	40	50	60	70	80	90	100
Very Hi											
High											
Average											
Low											
Very Lo											

Figure A.6

What is your present level of satisfaction with your *social* domain?

What would you like to change?

What would you have to do to initiate a change?

TRANSPORTATION DOMAIN

The Transportation domain includes all forms of mobility, including walking, bicycles, wheelchairs, cars, taxis, buses, boats, airplanes and any other form of transportation.

Ages	0	10	20	30	40	50	60	70	80	90	100
Very Hi											
High											
Average											
Low											
Very Lo											

Figure A.7

What is your present level of satisfaction with your *transportation* domain?

What would you like to change?

What would you have to do to initiate a change?

STEEP Scanning Worksheet
Chapter 6

	World	National	Local
Social			
Technology			
Economic			
Ecologic			
Political			

Figure A.8

LIFE EVENTS WORKSHEET
CHAPTER 7

Use the following worksheet to list events that you anticipate in your life during the life stage for which you are going to plan. Use the forces listed in the Domains column as reminders for events.

Domains And Sub-forces	High probability, high impact events in your life	Stake-holders events	Wild card events
Activities School, training Career, work Sports, hobbies Religion			
Finances Income, investments Expenses, debt			
Health Condition Medication Care			
Housing Home Community Country, region			
Social Family Friends Community			
Transportation Mobility Personal, auto Public			

Figure A.9

Personal Values Worksheet
Chapter 8

Values- what's important to you? This worksheet asks you to compare and rank your values. In the Rank column, select the value that is most important to you and enter the number 1. Then pick the second, third and on to the end of your list. For future reference, list the values in numerical order in the last column.

Value	Rank	List your Values in order of importance to you	Rank
Career			1
Professional relationships			2
Recognition			3
Power or influence			4
Income			5
Financial security			6
Net worth			7
Family			8
Family activities			9
Personal/family image			10
Ethics/principles			11
Religion			12
Independence			13
Contribution to others			14
Challenge/risk			15
Geographic location			16
Health			17
			18
			19
			20

Figure A.10

SWOT WORKSHEETS
CHAPTER 9

Strengths and Weaknesses

Internal	Strengths (Knowledge, abilities, skills, experience)	Weaknesses (Knowledge, abilities, skills)
Activities		
Finance		
Health		
Housing		
Social		
Transport (Mobility)		

Figure A.11

Opportunities

External Opportunities	Global	National	Local
Social			
Technology			
Economy			
Ecology			
Politics			

Figure A-12

Threats

External Threats	Global	National	Local
Social			
Technology			
Economy			
Ecology			
Politics			

Figure A-13

SCENARIO WORKSHEETS
CHAPTER 10

Forces and factors	Continuation of the Present scenario
Activities	
Finances	
Health	
Housing	
Social	
Transportation	
Goals, plans & values	

Figure A-14

Forces and factors	Best Plausible scenario
Activities	
Finances	
Health	
Housing	
Social	
Transportation	
Goals, plans & values	

Figure A-15

Forces and factors	Aspirational scenario
Activities	
Finances	
Health	
Housing	
Social	
Transportation	
Goals, plans & values	

Figure A-16

Forces and factors	Wild Card scenario
Activities	
Finances	
Health	
Housing	
Social	
Transportation	
Goals, plans & values	

Figure A-17

Forces and factors	Worst Plausible scenario
Activities	
Finances	
Health	
Housing	
Social	
Transportation	
Goals, plans & values	

Figure A-18

VISION WORKSHEETS
CHAPTER 15

Worksheet	Your vision for each domain for this stage
Activities What do you want to do? Education? Career? Travel? Sport? Religion?	
Finances What's important financially? Income? Net worth? Insurance? Estate?	
Health How do you see your health? What care will you need?	
Housing Where will you live?	
Social Who will be close to you? What groups will be important?	
Transportation How will you be transported?	

Figure A-19

VISION STATEMENT

Write in one sentence your vision of where you want your life to be at the end of your next life stage.

Now take this one more step. What do you want in your future for the rest of your life, beyond the next life stage? Do you want a long life? A healthy life? A close family throughout life? What will be important in retirement? What will be most important to you at the end of your life?

STRATEGIES FOR YOUR FUTURE
CHAPTER 16

A strategy is simply one way to do something. Chess is a game of strategies in which the player with the best strategies will probably win. You are looking for strategies to achieve your vision of the future, so spend some time thinking about how to devise the best strategy to achieve your vision.

Domains	Strategies to achieve goals, mission and vision	Strategies to avoid or reduce impacts of probable events
Activities		
Finances		
Health		
Housing		
Social		
Transportation		

Figure A-20

ACTION PLANS FOR YOUR FUTURE
CHAPTER 17

Now you must turn your strategies into actions. What actions must you take, starting today, to achieve your preferred future over the next ten years? What is the best sequence for those actions?

Year	Actions to be taken Activities-Finances-Health-Housing-Social -Transportation
2011	
2012	
2013	
2014	
2015	
2016	
2017	
2018	
2019	
2020	
2021	
2022	
2023	
2024	
2025	

Figure A-21

BACKCASTING

Year	Actions to be taken Activities-Finances-Health-Housing-Social -Transportation
2025	
2024	
2023	
2021	
2020	
2019	
2018	
2017	
2016	
2015	
2014	
2013	
2012	
2011	
2010	

Figure A-22

VULNERABILITY ANALYSIS
CHAPTER 18

	Vulnerabilities	Risk reduction
Activities		
Finances		
Health		
Housing		
Social		
Transportation		

Figure A-23

GAP ANALYSIS
CHAPTER 18

	Plan	Potential gap	Possible solution
Activities			
Finances			
Health			
Housing			
Social			
Transportation			

Figure A-24

THE PERSONAL FUTURES WHEEL
CHAPTER 18

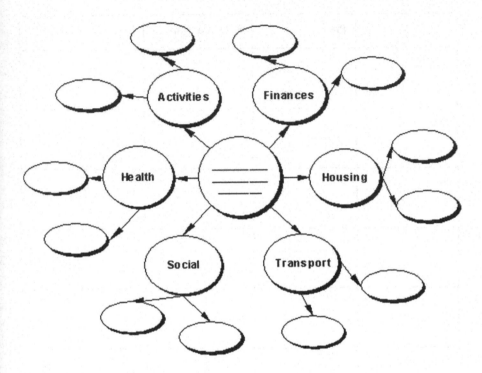

Figure A-25

CONTINGENCY PLANNING
CHAPTER 19

What happens if one of your Wild Card scenarios occurs? Or the Worst Plausible scenario? Develop contingency plans to deal with these.

Wild card or Worst Plausible event	Strategy (how will I deal with this event?)	Plan (what actions will I take to deal with this?)

Figure A-26

Use the strategy column to identify your general approach to dealing with this wild card or high impact event. In the Plan column, you can provide details for accomplishing your strategy.

References

This section provides references that are mentioned within the chapters, but also lists many of the authors and publications that influenced my writing of these chapters. In most cases the references are based on business or organizational futures and will provide more detail on the method or concept described in the chapter.

Chapter 1 Everyone Wants to Know the Future!

Bell, Wendell. *Foundations of Futures Studies: Human Science for a New Era*. New Brunswick: Transaction Publishers, 1997.

Cornish, Edward. *Futuring: The Exploration of the Future*. Bethesda: World Future Society, 2004.

De Geus, Arie. P. "Planning as Learning." *Harvard Business Review*, no. March-April (1988): 70-74.

Hines, Andy and Bishop, Peter, ed. *Thinking About the Future*. Washington, DC: Social Technologies, 2006.

May, Graham. *The Future is Ours*. Westport: Prager, 1996.

Wheelwright, Verne. *Personal Futures: Foresight & Futures Studies for Individuals*, (Ph.D. thesis).Harlingen, TX: Personal Futures Network. 2006,

Chapter 2 A Map to Your Future: Stages of Your Life

Erikson, Eric. *Identity and the Life Cycle*. New York: W.W. Norton & Co., 1980.

Wheelwright, Verne. 'Your Map to the Future', in *Tackling Tomorrow Today*, ed. Arthur B. Shostak. Langhorne, PA.: Chelsea House Publishers, 2004,

Chapter 3 The People in Your Future

Strauss, William and Howe, Neil. *Generations: The History of America's Future 1584 to 2069*. New York: William Morrow and Co., 1991.
Strauss, William and Howe, Neil. *Millennials Rising*. New York: Vintage Books, 2000.
Wheelwright, Verne. *A Personal Futures Workbook*. Harlingen: Personal Futures Network, www.personalfutures.net. 2008.

Chapter 4 Trends and Forces: Anticipating Change in Your Life

Groff, Linda. "Models of Change, with Examples of Key Issues in the Futures Studies Field." In *Thinking Creatively in Turbulent times*, ed. Howard Didsbury. Bethesda: World Future Society, pp. 83-104. 2004.
Schwartz, Peter. *The Art of the Long View*. New York: Currency Doubleday, 1991.

Chapter 5 Forces in Your Life: Past, Present and Future

Taylor, Charles W. "Creating Strategic Visions" *Futures Research Quarterly*,. Winter, (1991): 21-37.

Chapter 6 Forces That Shape Your Worlds: Global, National and Local

Canton, James., *The Extreme Future*, New York: Plume,. 2007.
Penn, Mark J. *Microtrends*. New York: Twelve, 2007.
The Millennium Project. "*Global Challenges for Humanity*" Available from http:www.millennium-project.org, 2010.

Chapter 7 Events That Will Change Your Life

Holmes, Thomas and Rahe, Richard. 'The Social Readjustment Rating Scale,' *Journal of Psychosomatic Research*, 11 no. 2 (1967): 213-218.
Miller, M. & Rahe, R. H. "Life Changes scaling for the 1990s." *Journal of Psychosomatic Research*43, no. 3 (1997): 279-292.
Schwartz, Peter. *The Art of the Long View*. New York: Currency Doubleday, 1991.

Chapter 8 Your Values Will Guide Your Future

Smith, Hyrum W. *What Matters Most.* New York: Simon and Schuster, 2000.

Morrisey, George L. *Creating Your Own Future.* San Francisco: Berrett-Koehler Publishers, 1992.

Chapter 9 Realistically You: Strengths, Weaknesses, Opportunities and Threats

Glenn, Jerome C. and Gordon, Theodore J. eds. *Futures Research Methodology,* Washington: American Council for the United Nations University, 2009.

Manktelow, James. "Personal SWOT Analysis." MindTools.com. www. mindtools.com/pages/artpages/article/icle/newTMC_05_1.htm

Chapter 10 Scenarios: How Futurists Explore Alternative Futures

Bezold, Clem. "Aspirational Futures." *Journal of Futures Studies,* vol. 13, no. 4 (2009) 81-90.

Gordon, Adam. *Future Savvy.* New York: AMACOM, 2009.

Inayatullah, Sohail. "Six Pillars: futures thinking for transforming." *Foresight,* vol. 10, no. 1 (2008) 4-21.

Kaivo-oja, Jari. "Scenario Learning and Potential Sustainable Development Processes in Spatial Contexts: Towards Risk Society or Ecological Modernization Scenarios." *Futures Research Quarterly,* vol. 17, no. 2, (2001) 33-55.

Van der Heijden, Kees. *Scenarios.* West Sussex: John Wiley & Sons, Ltd., 2006.

Chapter 11 Building Your Basic Scenario

Chermack, Thomas J., Lynham, Susan A. and Ruona, Wendy E. A. 'A Review of Scenario Planning Literature', *Futures Research Quarterly,* vol. 17, no. 2, (2001) 7-31.

Chapter 12 Driving Forces Will Change the Directions of Your Scenarios

Schwartz, Peter. *The Art of the Long View*. New York: Currency
Doubleday, 1991.
Taleb, Nassim Nicholas. *The Black Swan*. New York: Random House,
2007.

Chapter 13 Telling Stories About Your Future

Cascio, Jamais. "Futures Thinking: Writing Scenarios." *Fast Company*.
Available from: http://www.fastcompany.com/1560416/futures-
thinking-writing-scenarios. (03/15/10).

Chapter 14 Personal Strategic Planning

Mintzberg, Henry, Ahlstrand, Bruce and Lampel, Joseph. *Strategy Safari*.
New York: The Free Press, 1998.
Morrisey, George. L. *Creating Your Own Future*. San Francisco: Berrett-
Koehler Publishers. 1992.

Chapter 15 A Vision of Your Future

Senge, Peter and others. *The Fifth Discipline: The Art and Practice of the
Learning Organization*, New York: Doubleday, 1990.

Chapter 16 Strategies to Achieve Your Vision

De Geus, Arie. P. "Planning as Learning." *Harvard Business Review*, no.
March-April (1988): 70-74.
Goodstein, L. D., Nolan, T. M. and Pfeiffer, J. W. *Applied Strategic
Planning* San Francisco: Pfeiffer & Company, 1992.
Mintzberg, Henry. *The Rise and Fall of Strategic Planning*. New York:
Free Press, 1994.

Chapter 17 Creating Your Action Plan

Hines, Andy and Bishop, Peter, ed. *Thinking About the Future*.
Washington, DC: Social Technologies, 2006.

Chapter 18 Analyzing Your Plan

Goodstein, L. D., Nolan, T. M. and Pfeiffer, J. W. *Applied Strategic Planning* San Francisco: Pfeiffer & Company, 1992.

Chapter 19 Wild Cards and Contingency Plans

Barber, Marcus. "Wildcards—Signals from a Future Near You." *Journal of Futures Studies*, vol. 11, no. 1, (2006), 75-94.
Peterson, John L. *Out of the Blue*. Arlington: Arlington Institute, 1997.
Taleb, Nassim Nicholas. *The Black Swan*. New York: Random House, 2007.

Chapter 20 Living With Your Plan

Wheelwright, Verne. *A Personal Futures Workbook*. Harlingen: Personal Futures Network, www.personalfutures.net. 2008.

Chapter 21 The Long Term Perspective in Your Life and Your Career

Kouzes, James M. and Posner, Barry Z. *The Leadership Challenge*, San Francisco: Jossey Bass/Pfeiffer, 2002.
Meadows, D. H. *Thinking in Systems*. White River Junction VT.: Chelsea Green, 2008.

COLLEGES AND UNIVERSITIES OFFERING PROGRAMS OR COURSES IN FORESIGHT AND FUTURES STUDIES

Following is a list of colleges and universities that offer classes or degree programs in Foresight and Futures Studies. The listings in **bold face** indicate Masters level degree programs. The other listings may indicate a single class or multiple courses in Futures, either undergraduate or graduate.

Web sites are listed, but sometimes it is difficult to find anything relating to either Foresight or Futures Studies. You may have to find a "Contact us" page and send an email requesting information about Foresight and Futures Studies. In some schools, classes in Futures Studies are offered because a knowledgeable professor or instructor is available. If that person leaves, the class may end, so you will find changes in this list.

	School	Web site
United States	Anne Arundel Community College	www.aacc.edu
	Binghamton State University of New York	www.binghamton.edu
	California Inst. of Integral Studies	www.ciis.edu/
	Cal. State University, Dominguez Hills	www.csudh.edu
	Carnegie Mellon University	www.cmu.edu
	Case Western Reserve University	www.case.edu
	Colorado State University	www.drexel.edu
	Duke University	www.duke.edu
	Florida State University	www.fsu.edu
	Fullerton College	www.fullcoll.edu
	George Washington University	www.gwu.edu
	Harvard University	www.harvard.edu
	JFK University	www.jfku.edu
	Massachusetts Institute of Technology	www.mit.edu
	Monterey Institute of International Studies	www.mis.edu
	Northern Arizona University	www.nau.edu
	Pardee RAND Graduate School	www.prgs.edu
	Pepperdine University	www.pepperdine.edu

Portland State University	www.pdx.edu
Princeton University	www.princeton.edu
Regent University	www.regent.edu
San Diego Community College	www.sdcc.edu
Santa Clara University,	www.scu.edu
School for International Training	www.sit.edu
Singularity University	www.singularityu.org
Stanford University	www.stanford.edu
Tufts University	www.tufts.edu
Union Institute and University	www.tui.edu
University of Arizona	www.arizona.edu
University at Buffalo (SUNY)	www.buffalo.edu
University. of Advancing Technology	www.uat.edu
University of California Berkeley	www.berkeley.edu
University. of Cincinnati	www.uc.edu
University of Denver	www.du.edu
University of Hawaii at Manoa	www.futures.hawaii.edu
University of Houston	www.centraluh.edu
University of Kansas	www.ku.edu
University of Memphis	www.memphis.edu
University of Minnesota	www.umn.edu
University of Notre Dame	www.nd.edu
University of Pennsylvania	www.upenn.edu
University of Pittsburgh	www.pitt.edu
University of Washington	www.washington.edu
University of Southern California	www.usc.edu
Virginia Tech	www.vt.edu
William and Mary	www.wm.edu
Yale University	http://yale.edu

Argentina	Universidad Nacional de La Plata	www.unlp.edu.ar
	University of Palermo	www.palermo.edu.ar
Australia	Swinburne University of Technology	www.swineburne.edu.au
	Australian Catholic University	www.acu.edu.au
	Curtin University of Technology	www.curtin.edu.au
	Deakin University	www.deakin.edu.au
	Queensland University of Tech.	www.qut.edu.au
	University of the Sunshine Coast	www.usc.edu.au
Belgium	Free University of Brussels (VUB)	www.vub.ac.be
Brazil	Pontificia Universidade Catolica of Sao Paulo	www.puc.br
Canada	Ontario College of Art and Design	www.ocad.ca
Canada	Simon Fraser University	www.harbor.sfu.ca
Colombia	Universidade Externado de Colombia	http://portal.uexternado.edu.co
Costa Rica	United Nations University for Peace	www.upeace.org
Ecuador	ESPE	www.espe.edu.ec
Estonia	University of Tartu	www.ut.ee
Estonia	Tallinn University of Educational Sciences	www.ttut.ee
Europe	University of Malta	www.strategicfutures.eu
Finland	Finland Futures Academy	www.tvanet.fi
	Finnish Futures Research Center	www.tse.fi
France	EDHEC, Theseus-EDHEC Program.	www.edhec.edu
	Conservetoire National des Arts et Metiers	www.cnam.fr
	Université de Paris I/La Sorbonne	www.paris-sirbonne.fr
Germany	Technical University of Hamburg	www.tu-hamburg.de
	University of Applied Sciences Magdeburg	www.hsmagdeburg.de
Ghana	University of Cape Coast	www.uccghana.net
Hungary	Corvinus University of Budapest	www.uni-corvinus.hu
India	University of Kerala	www.keralauniversity.edu
Iran	Imam Khomeini International University	www.ikiu.ac.ir
Ireland	Dublin Inst. of Technology	www.dit.ie
Israel	Ben Gurion University of the Negev	www.bgu.ac.il

	Tel Aviv University School of Engrg.	www.telavivuniv.org
	Bar-Ilan University	www.biu.ac.il
Italy	Leonardo Da Vinci Online University	www.unidav.it
	Pontifical Gregorian University	www.unigre.urbe.it
Japan	Aichi University	http:www.aici-u.ac.jp
	Future University Hakodate	www.fun.ac.jp
	Kyoto University	www.kyoto-u.ac.jp
Malasia	University of Malaya	www.um.edu.my
	University Sains Malaysia	www.usainsgroup.com
Mexico	Monterrey Inst. of Tech	www.itesm.mx
	Universidad Regiomontana	www.ur.mx
	Universidad Nacional Autónoma de México	www.unam.mx
	Universidad del Valle de Mexico	www.umvnet.edu
Netherlands	Leiden University	www.leiden.edu
Norway	BI Norwegian School of Management	www.bi.no
	Norwegian University of Science and Tech.	www.svt.ntnu.no
Pakistan	Pakistan Futuristics Foundation and Institute	www.crm.sdnpk.org
Peru	ESAN, Grad. School of Business Admin.	www.esan.edu.pe
Philippines	University of St. La Salle	www.usls.edu.ph
Portugal	Technical University of Lisbon	www.utl.pt
Romania	Babes Bolyai University	www.ubbcluj.ro
Russia	Moscow State University	www.msu.ru
Singapore	Minerva School	www.minervaschool.com
	INSEAD, Asia Campus	www.insead.edu
	Nanyang Tech University	www.ntu.edu.sg
South Africa	University of Stellenbosch	www.sun.ac.za
South Korea	KAIST	www.keist.edu
Spain	University of Alicante	www.us.es
	University of Deusto in San Sebastián	www.duesto.es
Sweden	Goteborg University	www.gu.se
	Royal Inst. of Technology (KTH).	www.kth.se
Taiwan	Tamkang University	www.foreign.tku.edu.tw

248

	Fo Guang University	www.fgu.edu.tw
United Kingdom	Bath Spa University	www.bathspa.ac.uk
	Cardiff University.	www.cardiff.ac.uk
	Lancaster University	www.lancs.ac.uk
	Leeds Metropolitan University	www.lmu.ac.uk
	London Business School	www.london.ac.uk
	University of Cambridge	www.cam.ac.uk
	University of Hertfordshire,	www.herts.ac.uk
	University of Manchester	www.manchester.ac.uk
	University of Teesside	www.tees.ac.uk
	University of Oxford	www.ox.ac.uk
	University of Strathclyde	www.strath.ac.uk
	University of Sussex	www.sussex.ac.uk
Venezuela	University Central de Venezuela	www.ucv.ve

Index

About the Author

After a successful career in his own business in international trade, Verne Wheelwright went back to school. He enrolled at the University of Houston-Clear Lake in Studies of the Future, where he hoped to learn long term perspective and thinking. After earning his Masters degree, Wheelwright felt that the concepts and methods he had learned were extremely valuable, but that they were designed for large businesses and organizations.

Convinced that futures methods were not only effective, he believed they were also scalable—that these methods would be just as valuable to individuals and small businesses as they had been for decades to large organizations around the world. To prove that scalability, he enrolled in PhD research at Leeds Metropolitan University. Now Dr. Wheelwright, his dissertation Personal Futures: Foresight and Futures Studies for Individuals clearly demonstrated the scalability of the concepts and methods practiced by professional futurists worldwide.

Workshops and lectures further demonstrated the practical value and usability of personal futures methods to individuals. Wheelwright's Personal Futures Workbook has been adopted as a text in colleges and universities and thousands of copies have been distributed in several languages. The Workbook is now offered as a free download at www.personalfutures.net, and has been recently updated to be used with It's Your Future … Make it a good one!

Wheelwright is an active member of the Association of Professional Futurists, the World Future Society, and the World Futures Studies Federation. He chairs the APF committee that recognizes student work in Foresight and Futures Studies at universities worldwide and is a regular speaker at World Future Society conferences. Wheelwright has contributed a number of articles to international journals and other publications. After taking a year off to write this book, he plans to resume speaking and lecturing about the values that futures methods offer individuals and small businesses.

If you have questions, comments or suggestions about Personal Futures or about this book, you can contact the author by email at verne@personal-futures.net.